The Holy Spirit

IMPERATIVE

A Renewed Emphasis on the Person, Power, and Ministry Of the Holy Spirit

"Whenever and wherever the Church has been truly effective, there has been an emphasis upon the person and ministry of the Holy Ghost. The Holy Ghost is the executive administrator of the Kingdom. While the Word is the intelligence of the Kingdom, the Holy Spirit is the power. New Testament preaching is inseparable from the ministration of the Holy Ghost. We must remember that the Kingdom is not simply in word but in power. Christianity without the supernatural would simply be another philosophy. But it is not!"

Archbishop Kirby Clements - April 2019

Daniel C. Rhodes, MDiv

ISBN: 9798681761426

Destiny Navigators, LLC
Johns Creek, GA

www.DestinyNavigators.org
DanCRhodes@DestinyNavigators.org

Dedication

I dedicate this book to Archbishop Kirby Clements, who is a prophetic voice to the nations, the saints, and all Christian leaders in Christ's Church. His ever-present emphasis on the power and ministry of the Holy Spirit is the inspiration for this book.

I dedicate this book to my kind, loving, and gentle wife, Sheila, whose faith, ministry, and spiritual gifts come alive whenever and wherever she senses the presence of the Holy Spirit at work.

I dedicate this book to all pastors, bishops, church leaders, and the saints who hunger for the supernatural working of the Holy Spirit in their ministries and lives.

Acknowledgments

As always, I am greatly indebted to all my professors, mentors, pastors, theologians, and seasoned men and women of God who have deposited their wisdom and experience into my life. But most of all, I am grateful to the Lord for adding His wisdom to all that I have seen and experienced.

Without question, deep appreciation and gratitude are given to our youngest daughter, Anna Lindsey. Her creative and skillful assistance in copy-editing this work for grammatical correctness and flow of thought is irreplaceable. I am especially honored for Anna to work on this project with me because she and her family live what I write, as does our oldest daughter, Jenny Querubin, and her family.

Contents

PROLOGUE:
The Holy Spirit Imperative

There are books that bring historic events into our present world; and this is one. This is a strategic blend of scholarship and practicality. In an age of information and technology, this work awakens a sensitivity to the person and work of the Holy Spirit. The sections on "Fruit of the Spirit" and "Imperative" are priceless. Pastor Dan presents the Holy Spirit as *"the best friend we did not know we had."* This is a reference work that will invite you to read its pages many times.

Kirby Clements, DDS, MScD
Presiding Archbishop of the International Communion of Charismatic Churches www.TheICCC.org

---

If you are holding this book, you have a desire to understand the Holy Spirit and His workings in and through your own life. As you read these chapters, you will feel the heart of the author, a teacher of the Bible who carries a passion to make truths known that are applicable in the life of every believer in Jesus Christ. Pastor Dan Rhodes and his wife, Sheila, live what they are sharing with you.

God is Spirit. The Holy Spirit is God's Spirit at work to manifest all things according to God's desire and original plan. He is revealed to us in the person of Jesus - God in the flesh - who is the ultimate interpreter of Scripture and the perfect demonstration of the redeemed and Spirit filled Christian. Through the presence of and the empowerment of the Holy Spirit, God's Church, His people continue the ministry of Christ in the earth and fulfill God's original plan for His ultimate reign through His eternal Kingdom.

We are introduced to the Spirit of God in Genesis 1:2 and His presence and activities are seen on every page of the Scripture. Of course, the Holy Spirit is imperative for God's will to be done on earth. No human effort alone is able to fulfill the divine mandates that have been given to those who have chosen to believe in Jesus Christ and make Him know. I have ministered in over 100 nations of the world, bringing the Good News of Jesus and His redemptive work to people of practically every culture, language, and religion. Literally millions of people have turned from their old ways of life, to the new life that is only found through the cleaning blood of Jesus. We have seen literally thousands of physical healing miracles, that confirm the message of Christ. Many of these new believers have then been empowered by the Holy Spirit and have continued the ministry of Christ through the same Holy Spirit that was given to Jesus (Acts 10:38) and then given to all of His followers (Acts 1-2). All of this increase of the Kingdom and the testimony of the resurrected Jesus among hurting humanity has been possible through the Holy Spirit. Imperative? A resounding yes!

It is our prayer that you will experience a fresh empowerment of the Holy Spirit as you read this book so that you will see the miracles, signs and wonders through your own life that occurred through the life and example of Jesus! You can. ***The Holy Spirit Imperative!*** That's the plan!

Bishop LaDonna Osborn, D.Min.
President and CEO of Osborn Ministries International
www.osborn.org

I - The <u>Person</u> of the Holy Spirit

THE MYSTERY OF THE GREAT TRIUNE GOD

As a boy, I grew up attending a Presbyterian church every Sunday. I vividly recall reciting the Apostle's Creed and singing the Doxology. Even from those early years, I knew God was a Trinity: Father, Son and Holy Spirit. But I never grasped the full knowledge of who they really are until much later in life.

Twenty years later, the Lord graciously filled me with His Spirit and called me to full-time Christian ministry. With notebook and pen in hand, I sat in my first Systematic Theology class in seminary with all the expectation of a child at Christmas. ***That was when I learned the biblical reality of the great Triune God and their covenants of redemption and grace toward fallen humanity.*** Indeed, the Trinity is the central mystery of the Christian Faith. Our finite human minds can never fully understand their existence as **<u>One God</u>**, yet three Persons. Though the word "Trinity" never appears in the Old or New Testaments, its reality appears throughout the entire Christian Bible. In seminary, I learned the breadth of who They are and what They do.

Other monotheistic faiths (Judaism and Islam) also believe there is only one God (Deut. 6:4). And, indeed, there is! This is evident in the Hebrew scriptures and the writings of Muhammad (some of which came from the Hebrew scriptures). However, the Hebrew bible also speaks of the "Father" (Is. 63:16), the "Son" (Ps. 2:7, 12) and the "Holy Spirit." (Ps. 51:11). ***Judaism interprets this as a***

metaphorical relationship between God and the Jewish people. To them, the **Father** (Yahweh) is **God** who created all things. The **Son** will be the Jewish **human king** (Messiah) who will liberate the Jews from evil injustice and usher in the Messianic age of peace. And the **Holy Spirit** is the **divine force** and **influence** of Yahweh over the universe and God's creation.

In fact, the theologians of the early Christian church also struggled understanding the reality of the "Three-in-One" God. But the biblical evidence was too great to be ignored or explained away. It took until the 5th Century A.D. for a Christian creed to be written that established the orthodox view of the Great Triune God.

> *"The Father is God, the Son is God, and the Holy Spirit is God. And yet they are not three gods, but one God...The glory equal, the majesty co-eternal." - Athanasius Creed*

> **The Holy Spirit Imperative**
>
> **Without the work of each Person, including the Holy Spirit, the redemption of our souls from sin and the devil would be impossible.**

One of the challenges with which we all struggle (and are guilty of) is defaulting to an attempt to define God in human term...***with human limitations.*** God is not like us! The Westminster Confession of Faith declares, *"God is Spirit, infinite, eternal and unchangeable."* We lack human ability and language to comprehend, much less describe, the eternal nature of God as the Trinity. ***Without the work of each Person, including the Holy Spirit, the redemption of our souls from sin and the devil would be impossible.***

Clothed in eternity before the foundation of the world, there was ***a divine counsel between all three Persons of the Great Triune God.*** Before the fall of humanity, the Father, the Son, and the Holy Spirit, knowing the tragedy that would befall the human race, predetermined how they would fulfill their plan of redemption (Eph. 1:3-14). *(God's foreknowledge is not His foreordination.)* In the great Trinitarian Covenant of Redemption, the **Father** is the originator of the decree, the **Son** voluntarily takes the place of Adam and Eve's fallen race, becoming the ultimate sacrifice for the sin of all mankind, and the **Holy Spirit** applies the saving work of the Son to the hearts of believers. ***Hence, redemption has its conception, implementation, and culmination secured with an irrevocable eternal covenant made by God Himself, who cannot lie.*** Thus, we refer to the Holy Spirit as the "Third Person" of the Trinity, not because of the preeminence of the others, but by virtue of how they apply their redemptive grace in the lives of sinful humanity. ***Therefore, when Jesus bore the weight of our sin, so did the whole Godhead (Col. 2:9), including the Holy Spirit.***

THE HOLY SPIRIT IS A "PERSON"

As a Sy-fi fan, I've always enjoyed watching the George Lucas films, "Star Wars." And, of course, one of the great memorable quotes is, *"May the Force Be with You!"* This referred to an impersonal force of the universe that both good and evil people could tap into to have power over their opponents. ***In stark contrast, the Holy Spirit is not an impersonal "force" or "influence" in human lives, and neither is He just another "manifestation" of God.***

The Holy Spirit is one of the "Persons" of the Trinity. ***By Persons, we mean that all three have distinct, separate, rational, and moral*** *identities. Just as with the Father and the Son, the Holy Spirit personally cares for you and seeks your fellowship and worship (John 4:23; 2 Cor. 13:14; Philip. 2:1).* Beyond our finite understanding, God is a complex manifold being with one undivided divine essence in which there are three Persons. As mentioned above, to each Person of the Trinity belongs their undivided essence with the full attributes of God. Thus, the Father is God; the Son is God; and the Holy Spirit is God. Each Person of the Trinity eternally existed prior to creation, and, as mentioned before, each has unique external acts in regard to creation and redemption.

> The Holy Spirit Imperative
>
> **Just as with the Father and the Son, the Holy Spirit personally cares for you and seeks your fellowship and worship.**

"PERSONALITY TRAITS" OF THE HOLY SPIRIT

The Holy Spirit is not human; He is God! Yet, as a "Person" of the Trinity, there are consistent spiritual characteristics that further describe who He is, how He deals with us, and how we must treat Him. Unless we are continually mindful of this, we can easily offend God and jeopardize His kind intentions toward us. Here are a few of the Holy Spirit's "Personality Traits":

1. **The Holy Spirit Is Sovereign.** Because He is God, His acts are sovereign, and no one can rescind His plans or purposes (Is. 14:27; 46:9-11). When He distributes spiritual gifts to us, He does so just as **He wills**, not as we desire (1 Cor. 12:11). Yet, there is no conflict of wills between the Persons of the Trinity, for they are one and of the same agenda: to reveal Himself to us and restore us back to Himself.

2. **The Holy Spirit Is Love.** Since God is love (1 John 4:16), the Holy Spirit (who is God) also pours out His love in the hearts of believers (Rom. 5:5). And through His power in us, we can love others with God's love (Gal. 5:22).

3. **The Holy Spirit Is Gentle and Patient (Gal. 5:22).** When the Father draws people to Christ and when Christ draws them to Himself (John 6:44; 12:32), He does so by His Spirit who patiently waits for our response.

4. **The Holy Spirit Honors the Father and the Son of God.** He never draws attention to Himself, but always prefers the other Persons of the Trinity (John 15:26; Rom. 8:15-16). This is why Jesus is so protective of Him (Luke 12:10).

5. **The Holy Spirit Freely Gives to Us That Which Is His.** The spiritual gifts that the Holy Spirit gives to us aren't ours; **they are His** in us (1 Cor. 12:7-11). Even the fruit of the Holy Spirit is His character in us (Gal. 5:22-23).

6. **But, Don't Underestimate His Kindness. The Holy Spirit Can Be Easily Grieved.** Deliberate rebellion against God grieves the Holy Spirit and can cause Him to become as an enemy who chastens (Is. 63:10). Likewise, a believer's bitterness, rage, anger, brawling, slander, and malice toward one another grieves God's Spirit (Eph. 4:29-32). This is because the Holy Spirit has sealed our redemption in Christ, and He expects us to act toward one another accordingly.

7. **The Holy Spirit Is Protective.** He awakens our conscience to keep us from drifting off God's course for us. And when we fail, He becomes our "Advocate" (Defense Attorney) who represents the atoning work of Jesus (John 14:16-17).

THE HOLY SPIRIT IS IMPERATIVE IN OUR LIVES

Again, I will be forever grateful for the superlative educational training I received from the small Presbyterian (PCA) seminary I attended in 1978. They imparted to me a high regard for Scripture and an orthodox Christian theology that equally honors all three Persons of the Great Triune God. Therefore, when I speak of "The Holy Spirit Imperative," I'm not at all diminishing our emphasis on the Father and the Son. ***I'm encouraging all of us to place equal emphasis on the Holy Spirit as we do with the Father and the Son, for all three are God.***

Christian preaching and teaching rightly and biblically directs us to *"fix our eyes on Jesus (**the Son of God**), the author and perfecter of faith, who for the joy set before Him endured the cross, despising the shame, and has sat down at the right hand of the throne of God."* (Heb. 12:2). Yet, Jesus taught us to pray to the **Father** (Matt. 6:9), who is the Originator of all things. Even His name, "Father," expresses His loving relationship, care, and protection of a father for his children. As Earn Baxter, a great theologian and preacher of the 20th century, once said, *"The Holy Spirit is the existential Jesus in the world."* In other words, through the Holy Spirit, Jesus the Son of God, lives in us even in His absence. ***As such, it is IMPERATIVE that we see Him as more than just the spiritual "Gift-Giver" of 1 Corinthians 12. We must honor Him in our preaching, teaching and lives for the fulness of who He really is.***

> The Holy Spirit Imperative
>
> **He's more than just the spiritual "Gift-Giver" of 1 Corinthians12.**

II - The Power and Ministry of the Holy Spirit in the World

He Does More than You Think!

Across decades of my ministry, I've discovered that many people tend to be Myopic (short sighted), along with the added hindrance of Tunnel Vision (a very narrow point of view), when they consider the ministry of the Holy Spirit. Their view can be limited only to His work in Christian believers. And certainly, He empowers us to be Christ's witnesses in the world, and He bestows upon us the spiritual gifts of 1 Corinthians 12. ***Many don't stop to think that the power and ministry of the Holy Spirit is infinitely greater than they can possibly imagine. He spans the entire history of humanity and the world, even before time began.***

The Holy Spirit's Light Overcomes the Power of Evil's Darkness

We've all read this familiar passage in Gen. 1:2-4 many times:

> *"The earth was **formless and void**, and **darkness** was over the surface of the deep, and the **Spirit of God was moving** (hovering) over the surface of the waters." **Then God said, 'Let there be light'; and there was light.** God saw that the light was good; and **God separated the light from the darkness.**"*

This can certainly refer to God's process of creation. And it does. However, hidden in scriptural accounts are spiritual truths greater than the story itself. Consider the following biblical interpretations:

- **Formless, Void, and Darkness** - "Formless" and "Void" in Hebrew means chaos and empty. "Darkness" can describe the domain of evil (Col. 1:13). Since God did not create the world like this, it can refer to the insurrection of Lucifer who was cast to the earth bringing with him his kingdom of evil. (Rev. 12:7-9)

- **Spirit of God Was Moving (Hovering)** - This is the first time in Scripture we learn of the work of the Holy Spirit. Wherever there is the chaos and darkness of evil, the Holy Spirit hovers above it all to bring God's order and light.

- **God Said, "Let There Be light; and There Was Light"** - When the voice of God speaks, the power of the Holy Spirit accomplishes that which has been spoken. Light overcomes darkness, both naturally and spiritually. Just as Jesus, the Son of God, is God's spiritual light that overpowers evil's darkness (John 1:4-5), so is the Holy Spirit. ***His Light is God's reversal of chaos and darkness.***

- **God Separated the Light from the Darkness** - Here we see the principle of separation. Whenever God's Spirit shines spiritual light into a dark world, the distinction between good and evil becomes undeniable.

The Holy Spirit Imperative

His Presence "hovers" over your dilemmas to bring God's solution.

Therefore, it is IMPERATIVE to recognize and emphasize the power of the Holy Spirit's Light. Whenever darkness invades your personal world and life, you can rest assured that ***the Presence of the Holy Spirit is "hovering" over your dilemmas to bring God's solution.*** When He shines His Light on you, you can clearly see the path that leads you out of darkness into His marvelous Light (1 Pet. 2:9).

THE HOLY SPIRIT IS THE CREATIVE BREATH OF GOD

The second time we read of the Holy Spirit's work in Scripture is the account of the origin of the human race (Gen. 2:7). It was by the "Breath" (wind) of God that Adam became a living soul. When the Father and the Son "breathe" it most certainly involves the work of His Spirit. This is confirmed by Jesus when He "breathed" on His disciples and said, "Receive the Holy Spirit" (John 20:22). Again, when Jesus described the "New Birth" to Nicodemus, He said it can only happen by the Spirit, who is like "Wind" (John 3:5-8). Without the "Inbreathing" of the Holy Spirit, the "New Creation" in Christ could never happen. The Holy Spirit is the "Breath" of God that brings life to all things. ***And, He can even breathe life into discouraged hearts, lifeless dreams, and purposeless lives...when we humble ourselves and seek Him with all our heart. (John 6:63; Jer. 29:11-13).***

> **The Holy Spirit Imperative**
>
> **He breathes life into discouraged hearts, lifeless dreams, and purposeless lives.**

THE HOLY SPIRIT IS "GOD IN ACTION" ON EARTH (COMMON GRACE)

Common Grace is that general operation of the Holy Spirit whereby He, WITHOUT RENEWING THE HEART, exercises such a moral influence on mankind that sin is restrained, and order is maintained in social life. This also includes general blessings such as food, rain, and shelter even for unbelievers (Matt. 5:45; Luke 6:35). ***He originates, maintains, strengthens, and guides all life (organic, intellectual, and moral) toward God's ultimate purposes.***

THE HOLY SPIRIT HAS ALWAYS BEEN AT WORK ...EVEN BEFORE PENTECOST

The Holy Spirit is the Spirit of Enablement and Empowerment given to those called to a specific task, mission, and purpose in God's Kingdom. Before the redemptive work of Christ and Pentecost, enablement was usually temporary and occasional. In the Old Testament, He took possession and clothed men but did not permanently indwell them. This may have been because He would not set up His residence in a vessel that had not been permanently atoned to God. Here are some examples:

- Artistic design and the building of the Temple. (Ex. 31:3-5)
- Intellectual insight. (Job 32:8; Ex. 28:3)
- Qualifying men as leaders of people. (Num. 11:17; 27:16-19)
- Anointing rulers of Israel. (1 Sam. 11:6; 16:13)
- Enabling men to render judgment and fight enemies. (Judges 3:10; 11:29; 13:24-25)
- Anointing men for prophecy. (Num. 11:25; 24:2-3; 1 Sam. 10:5-6)
- Supernatural Empowerment. (Zech. 4:6-7; 1 Kings 18:12)
- Special Insight from God. (2 Sam. 23:2; Neh. 9:30)

III - The Power and Ministry of the Holy Spirit In Your Life

THE HOLY SPIRIT WAS WITH YOU...EVEN WHILE YOU WERE BEING FORMED FOR BIRTH

Years ago, I was ministering to a young Christian man who had become discouraged with himself, life, and God. Because of his personal turmoil, he questioned if the Lord was even aware of him. *"If God is with me,"* he complained, *"then why doesn't He do something to help me?"*

I began by asking him to read Psalm 139:15-16.

> *"My frame was not hidden from You, when I was made in secret, and skillfully wrought in the depths of the earth. Your eyes have seen my unformed substance; and in Your book were all written the days that were ordained for me, when as yet there was not one of them."*

Together we read Ps. 71:6 and Gal. 1:15 revealing that God called him to Himself, protected him, and led him even before he believed. And finally, we read Philip. 1:6, *"For I am confident of this very thing, that He who began a good work in you will perfect it until the day of Christ Jesus."*

> The Holy Spirit Imperative
>
> **He's your best Friend that you didn't know you had!**

I concluded by assuring him that God loves him and is forever aware of him. All he had to do was to open his heart with humility to God and His word, and the Holy Spirit would show him how to resolve his dilemmas. ***As he walked out the door, I reminded him, "The Holy Spirit is your best Friend that you didn't know you had!"***

Two Conflicting Residencies – Living in the Holy Spirit and Living in the World

I was teaching a class on the Holy Spirit and a student came to me after class with a dilemma. *"I'm confused,"* he said. *"How can I live in the Holy Spirit and at the same time live in an ungodly world? This isn't working very good for me. On one hand I'm following Christ and on the other I'm behaving like the world. I need help!"*

This is indeed a difficult dichotomy to navigate. Even the Apostle Paul recorded his struggle with this dilemma in Rom. 7:14-24. But, thank the Lord, he concluded his struggle by writing Rom. 7:25 and Rom. 8:1-2. Only Jesus can solve this impasse. His Substitutionary Atonement took our sin and gave us His righteousness (2 Cor. 5:21). ***But we can't stop with Jesus. Only by the power of the Holy Spirit can we even know who Jesus is and what He did for us (John 15:26; 16:13-15).***

However, we dare not assume that because we're forgiven, we can behave any way we want (Rom. 6:1-2). ***In fact, the Holy Spirit is your "Early Warning Sentry!"*** He's not your "conscience," but He can awaken your moral principles and remind you who you are in Christ and what He has redeemed you from (Eph. 4:17-24). This develops an inner

> The Holy Spirit Imperative
>
> He's your "Early Warning Sentry," awakening your conscience to repentance.

conflict between your flesh and God's righteous intentions for your life (Gal. 5:16–17). When His convicting influence brings ***godly sorrow*** in your heart, it produces repentance without regret (John 16:8; 2 Cor. 7:10). This is true for all of us, regardless of our titles or places in ministry. ***If it wasn't for the gracious work of the Holy Spirit, we'd drift off course from God and self-destruct on the rocks of foolish choices, decisions and actions.***

GOD'S DUAL STRATEGY: THE HOLY SPIRIT LIVING IN YOU...AND YOU LIVING IN THE HOLY SPIRIT

Many years ago, I was riding in a friend's car as he drove 20 mph over the speed limit, careened around corners, and rode the bumpers of cars in front of him. I clenched the door handle and stomped the floorboard as if there was brake pedal on my side of the car. I warned him of what might happen to us, but he ignored my warning and kept driving like a daredevil!

After that harrowing experience, I reflected on what had happened. Then I realized THE POWER OF LIVING IN THE HOLY SPIRIT. When He lives in you, He warns you from within. Unfortunately, you can ignore His warnings and still do what you want. ***But if you live in the Holy Spirit, He's in charge, steering your life, taking you where He knows you need to go, and obeying all the rules as you travel through life together.*** Scripture confirms both realities. Most definitely, when we are born again, the Holy Spirit lives in us forever (John 14:16-17; 2

> The Holy Spirit Imperative
>
> **When you live in the Holy Spirit, He's in charge, steering your life and taking you where He knows you need to go.**

Tim. 1:14). However, even when He lives in us, we can still grieve Him by our disobedience (Eph. 4:30; 1 Thess. 5:19). But at the same time, we live IN the Holy Spirit and IN Christ (Rom. 8:1; Rev. 1:10; 21:10). ***This means because we're inseparably united with the Holy Spirit and Jesus, we must endeavor to live a life of obedience to His righteous intentions.*** When this remarkable reality settles in your heart, it totally changes how you live. The reality is that we who are the redeemed don't have to ***try*** to live in the Holy Spirit. We already do! As soon as you sense the Holy Spirit's correction and direction from within, immediately respond with repentance and obedience. This doesn't mean we are trying to earn righteousness by good works; it means we're already righteous in Christ and we're endeavoring to live that way. When this happens, it confirms that He's in charge, steering your life, and taking you where He knows you need to go.

> The Holy Spirit Imperative
>
> **Because we're inseparably united with the Holy Spirit and Jesus, you must endeavor to live a life of obedience to His righteous intentions.**

THE HOLY SPIRIT IS YOUR "NAVIGATOR"

When I was a teenager, my Dad (who was my hero), taught me to fly small airplanes. I learned quickly that it's one thing to know where you want to go, but it's a whole different matter to find out how to get there. That's called navigation. It's the process of determining your current position, plotting a course to arrive at your destination, and calculating the distance traveled and the time it takes to arrive safely. That's great for flying airplanes or driving cars. But it doesn't work so well in spiritual matters.

That's why you need the Holy Spirit to navigate more than just one journey; you need Him to navigate your whole life!

One of the ways the Holy Spirit navigates is by His ***Providential Care*** over your life. He lovingly guides and sustains your destined purposes in Christ. *(By the way, God can, at His discretion, providentially care for people even before they're born again.)* **That was abundantly true for me!**

> **The Holy Spirit Imperative**
>
> **You need Him to navigate more than just one journey; you need Him to navigate your whole life!**

The Holy Spirit's Providential Care Means:

1. **He Provides for You:** God, in His infinite foreknowledge, knows what you need, even before you do (Matt. 6:8, 11, 32). When good opportunities and provisions seem to appear out of nowhere, ***that's the Holy Spirit's work!***

2. **He Preserves Your Life:** Because He knew you and His righteous intentions for you even when you were an embryo, He sustains your life and protects you from harm until you've completed your purpose on earth (Ps. 3:1-8; 2 Tim. 4:7, 17-18). As you look back across your life and reflect on dangers you escaped from, ***that was the Holy Spirit's work!***

3. **He Directs Your Paths:** God supernaturally governs paths, directs lives and points all who trust in Him toward God's destined purposes (Prov. 3:5-10; 16:9). However, you must be sensitive to His leading and yield to His wisdom. This can only happen when you know the difference between His voice and your own thoughts. When you can discern this, ***that's the Holy Spirit at work!***

4. **He Walks with You:** Because your purpose and assignment in God's Kingdom is greater than you can accomplish in your own strength, He accompanies you throughout life (Ex. 33:14-15; Deut. 31:6-8). As He walks with you, He's teaching you how to walk with character, integrity and wisdom. When you sense the "Wind" of God filling your sails, ***that's the Holy Spirit at work!***

5. **He's the Master of Timing and Coordination:** Beyond our human reasoning, the Holy Spirit can time and coordinate things to happen precisely when they should and as they should in order to further His purposes for your life (Gen. 22:13-14; Rom. 8:28). When situations are too inexplicable to be ordinary coincidences, ***it's the Holy Spirit at work!***

Another aspect of the Holy Spirit's supernatural navigation is preventing you from doing what you thought was a good thing. This is what happened to the Apostle Paul when he believed it was good for him to preach in a northern province of Asia (Acts 16:6-10). The wisdom of God is infinitely superior to our good plans. It could have been that danger or death awaited Paul in that region. Or perhaps that mission was reserved for someone else. Or, as the account unfolded, Macedonia needed the Gospel more than Phrygia and Galatia at that time. ***When the Holy Spirit is at work, a closed door from God is just as much His leading as an open door.***

THE HOLY SPIRIT IS YOUR "REVEALER"

I still recall the amazement and excitement I felt in seminary when spiritual truths became crystal clear. My professor "connected the spiritual dots" for me and, for the first time in my life, I saw reality from God's perspective. From that time until now, when I read the

Bible, the Holy Spirit reveals deeper and deeper truths about God, His character, His unconditional love for fallen humanity, and His work in the world. These truths continue to ignite my mind and fuel the zeal of my calling as a pastor and teacher of the word. Even now, passages I've read hundreds of times suddenly come alive, by the power of the Holy Spirit, with new revelations and understandings of God's grace and love for His people and for me. ***Since the Holy Spirit is the true author of God's word (2 Tim. 3:16; 2 Peter 1:20), He is the "Revealer" of all truths in Scripture as well as all spiritual realities.***

> <u>The Holy Spirit Imperative</u>
>
> **Since the Holy Spirit is the true author of God's word, He is the "Revealer" of all truths in Scripture as well as all spiritual realities.**

"Revealing" is an ongoing process. It has the connotation of "unveiling," like removing a cloth cover from a priceless painting. This can also be illustrated by drawing back the curtain to see all that's happening behind the stage of life. In the spiritual sense, "revelation" is God making known to us His marvelous mysteries that were previously hidden from our natural minds. To the unbeliever, the mysteries of God remain hidden from their understanding. But to us, who are the redeemed, they are the precious truths and power of God revealing Himself, His gracious plan for our lives, and His Kingdom (Matt. 13:11; 1 Cor. 1:18).

These Are Some of the Precious Truths the Holy Spirit <u>Continues</u> to Reveal to You Throughout Your Life and As You Grow in Christ.

- **He Reveals and Reminds You that Jesus Is Your Savior.** This is His prime mission (John 15:26; 16:14-15). You weren't aware of it, but you encountered the Holy Spirit even before Jesus. He opened your heart to reveal who Jesus is and what He has done for you. Without the Holy Spirit, you never would have been born again! Even after you are birthed into God's Kingdom, ***He continues to remind you afresh of Christ's indescribable gift that gave you eternal life.***

- **He Reveals Your Redeemed Identity in Christ.** Like with Peter, the Father (by the Holy Spirit) reveals to you that Jesus is the Christ, the Son of the Living God. He then reveals who you are, why you are alive and what your purpose is on earth. He even gives you a new name and a fresh start in life (Matt. 16:15-17; 2 Cor. 5:17).

- **He Reveals the Mind and Will of Christ.** The ultimate goal of Jesus is restoration. The Son of God came to earth to redeem you back to the Father through His Substitutionary Atoning work. Then, after giving you His righteousness, His will is for you to walk in that righteousness. This is the mind that you must continually have (1 Cor. 2:9-16; 1 Thess. 4:3-5). Just as Jesus intercedes for you, His will is for you to join Him in interceding for others (James 5:16).

- **He Reveals Your Spiritual Calling and Gifting.** The Holy Spirit reminds you that you are called out of darkness into His marvelous light. Along with all Christians, you are called to be an ambassador for Christ. Some have the specific callings of Eph. 4:11-16 to bring knowledge and maturity to the Body of Christ. Along with your calling, the Holy Spirit gives spiritual gifts to benefit all people. The Holy Spirit reveals and confirms your calling and gifts by the evidence of what they produce in people's lives for the glory of God. (1 Pet. 2:9; 2 Cor. 5:18; 1 Cor. 12:4-11).

- **He Reveals Words of Prophecy, Knowledge and Wisdom to Those Whom He Gives These Gifts.** If you've ever received a prophesy or words of knowledge or wisdom, you may have been shocked that they came through someone who knew nothing about you. The obvious conclusion is that only God could have revealed these things to the person who spoke to you. People cannot have this kind of intimate knowledge about the lives of others...unless God is involved. It's the Holy Spirit who reveals these powerful words to the heart of the one who is ministering to you. (1 Cor. 12:8-10).

- **He Reveals the Kingdom of God to You.** The reality of the Kingdom of God (His righteous rule in heaven and earth) is meaningless to the unbeliever. It's impossible for them to see (perceive by human senses) God's Kingdom unless they're "born from above" by the Holy Spirit. The barrier of unbelief bars their entrance into God's righteous Kingdom, and they're locked out (John 3:3-5). The moment you were spiritually born again, the Holy Spirit revealed God's vast Kingdom in which you will live forever. When you began walking in His Saving Grace, you learned that you were clothed with Jesus' **RIGHTEOUSNESS** *(Right standing with God).* Then you felt enveloped in **PEACE** *(no more fighting)* with God. Finally, you were filled with **JOY** because you were once lost in sin, and now you have eternal life...forever! This, my friend, was what Paul revealed to us in Romans 14:17 when he wrote, **"THE KINGDOM OF GOD IS *RIGHTEOUS*, *PEACE*, AND *JOY*...IN THE HOLY SPIRIT!"**

THE HOLY SPIRIT IS YOUR "SECRET PLACE" WITH THE LORD

When I first came to the saving knowledge of Christ, I was filled and overwhelmed by His love for me. It wasn't out of fear of going to Hell that I asked Jesus to come into my life. He just did it out of His amazing sovereign grace! I was overcome by the goodness of His Presence and lost in His unconditional love for me. Then I realized, throughout my whole life before Christ, He had always been there for me...protecting me, guiding me and rescuing me from dangers both seen and unseen! And beyond belief, I knew He had been patiently waiting for me to come to that life-changing day in Him! All I wanted to do was get quiet before the Lord and weep with joy and gratitude. And I did! I had found the "Secret Place" with God. It was sweet communion with the Father, the Son and the Holy Spirit. ***And now I know I will never be fully satisfied in life unless His Spirit continually beckons me to enter His sacred Presence in God's Secret Place (Song 2:10).*** There my soul is refreshed, and all things become clear. If this is what Heaven will be like, I have a small glimpse of what's waiting for all the redeemed who love Him and are called by Him to everlasting life.

> The Holy Spirit Imperative
>
> **I will never be fully satisfied in life unless His Spirit continues to beckon me to enter His sacred Presence in God's Secret Place.**

As said before, the Father is God, the Son is God, and the Holy Spirit is God...three Persons yet one God. When Jesus left the earth to return to the Father, they both sent the Holy Spirit to live forever with and in us. In Jesus' absence, the Secret Place is your place of quiet communion in the Presence of the whole Godhead. ***Since the Holy Spirit lives in us, our communion with Him is also with the Father and the Son.*** The nearness to God that you feel is His Spirit. The "Secret Place" is the Presence of the Spirit of God (Ps. 31:20).

The Holy Spirit Imperative

Since the Holy Spirit lives in us, our communion with Him is also with the Father and the Son.

The Secret Place is "Secret" because it's hidden from all who reject God. When psalmist wrote about *"Dwelling in the Secret Place of the Most High"* (Ps. 91:1), He was speaking of the protection that the Presence of the Lord gave him from his enemies. For us, as New Testament saints, it means so much more. ***Here's what you receive when you enter the Secret Place of the Holy Spirit. These are more reasons why He really is IMPERATIVE!***

- **He's Your Intimate Place with God** – No one knows you like God. He was with you when you were born and was close to you as you grew into adulthood. He knows your every thought, fear and need. In His Secret Place you have communion with the Father and the Son. ***There, He even shares His heart and thoughts with you*** (Ps. 139:17).

- **He's Your Confessing and Forgiving Place** – As a believer, the Holy Spirit discloses and applies the Savior's saving grace to your life. He sealed your soul with the validity of your redemption and forgiveness (Eph. 1:13). When you bring your sins to God, He takes your heartfelt confessions and declares to you that you are forgiven and cleansed from unrighteousness (1 John 1:9). ***Then, His Presence in you refreshes your soul with the knowledge of your forgiveness.***

- **He's Your Asking and Receiving Place** - With enthusiasm, we read the encouraging John 16:23 passage, *"If you ask the Father for anything in My name, He will give it to you."* Since your "Resident God" is the Holy Spirit, ***He hears your request and evaluates it according to God's will before the Father, the Son and the Holy Spirit grants it*** *(1 John 5:14-15).*

- **He's Your Comforting Place** - In life we experience joys and sorrows. When we encounter hardships, loneliness, and discouragements, we know that Jesus sent the Holy Spirit to help us. He is the "Comforter" (also translated as "Counselor, Helper, Advocate, and Intercessor") to be with us after Jesus returned to heaven (John 14:16-20). ***He comes alongside of us, walks with us, and comforts us with His counsel.***

- **He's Your Instruction and Counseling Place** - When you walk through dark valleys or life's dramas, you can be left with questions and confusion. The Holy Spirit has infinite knowledge, understanding and wisdom. ***Seek His counsel and He will teach you how to deal with your dilemmas and walk through them into His Light (Ps. 32:7–8; 1 Cor. 2:9-11).***

- **He's Your Praying and Intercession Place** - Paul explains a mystery. It's possible to pray with both your mind and with your spirit (1 Cor. 14:14-15). With the Holy Spirit's gift of tongues (spiritual language), you pray mysteries to God that only He understands (1 Cor. 14:2). When you don't know how to pray for someone (or for a complex issue in your life) the Holy Spirit helps you pray (and intercedes for you) according to the will of God (Rom. 8:26-27). ***The more you pray in the Spirit - the closer you are to God and the more He keeps you in alignment with His will.***

IV - The Power and Ministry of the Holy Spirit Through Your Life

When my wife, Sheila, and I entered the ministry, I had confidence that the Holy Spirit would minister to people through us. But I didn't know exactly what that would look like. As a teacher of the word, I believed He would work through His teaching gift in me and His calling on my life to help people better understand and apply scriptural truths to their lives (Eph. 4:11). And He does. But the wonderful surprise was to discover the Spiritual Gifts the Lord gave to my wife! ***When Sheila received the Baptism in the Holy Spirit, she was instantaneously filled with the power of God.*** Without being "coached," she suddenly began speaking in her prayer language (tongues) and praising God in her spirit. This was a foretaste of the kind of ministry she would have. Throughout our ministry together, Words of Knowledge and prophetic utterances flowed through her to strengthen, encourage, and comfort those to whom she ministered. ***I saw firsthand the authenticity of the 1 Corinthians 12:4-11 spiritual gifts with the demonstration of the Spirit and of power.***

THE DEMONSTRATION OF THE SPIRIT AND POWER THROUGH YOU

It's one thing (and a wonderful blessing) to speak and preach wise and persuasive words. Through this, the Holy Spirit applies spiritual truths to hearts to encourage people and bring them to a deeper relationship with the Lord. But it's a totally different matter to minister with the ***"Demonstration of the Spirit and of power, so that*** *the faith of people would not rest on the wisdom of men, but on the power of God" (1 Cor. 2:4-5).* However, Paul wrote that even in his teaching and preaching, he was revealing the wisdom of God's mysteries (1 Cor. 2:6-7). It's true, through the ministry of God's word, many are led to Christ and grow in their faith. But when the spiritual gifts of the Holy Spirit flow in a church service, they are **SIGN-GIFTS** from God that He is present and working with them. They introduce and bring people into His supernatural realm of His grace, love, and care for them. ***But without the manifestations of the Holy Spirit in a worship service, there is the missing dynamic of the supernatural working of God.***

> The Holy Spirit Imperative
>
> **Without the manifestations of the Holy Spirit in a worship service, there is the missing dynamic of the supernatural working of God.**

The 1 Cor. 12:4-11 Manifestations of the Holy Spirit Can Be Categorized as: 1) Revealing, 2) Speaking, and 3) Power Gifts.

1) THE HOLY SPIRIT'S "REVEALING" GIFTS

Sheila, and I were ministering in a local church in another state a few years ago. After I brought the word of God in teaching, Sheila came up to minister to the people by the Spirit. She spoke to a woman in the congregation whom she had never met or knew anything about. Sheila said to her, "I see you like a bird in a cage." *(Then there was a gasp that went across the whole congregation.)* Sheila continued speaking, "The door of the cage is open, but you won't come out because you're afraid. I see the hand of God reaching into the cage and beckoning you to come out through the open door. You come to the edge of the door, but you go back in. The Lord is saying to you, 'Come out and fly and be all that I've called you to be.'" After the service the pastor spoke to Sheila about this word she had given. The woman had been imprisoned for years and was struggling with many addictions. He had been counseling with her across the years. Then he said to Sheila, "If she heeds it, this was the word of God that will set her free!"

God knows everything about us. He knows our past, present, and future. He knows our successes and our failures. He knows our problems and the solutions to our dilemmas. He knows our heart's desires and His righteous destiny for our lives. He also knows wrong decisions that we're about to make and their consequences. Because He loves us, He warns us of impending dangers. And He knows the encouragement we need to not give up but to press forward in Christ. Because of God's love for His people, He may choose to give you His "Revealing Gifts" to encourage and show them how much He's aware of their lives. Through these gifts, He can reveal to your heart personal matters about an individual's life that you know nothing about. When they hear your words, **IT'S A SIGN TO THEM** that it must be God who revealed these things to you. This encourages believers, builds up their faith, and stirs their hearts to walk closer with the Lord. If it's an unbeliever, they'll know God is real, He's aware of them, and He loves them. ***Unless the Revealing Gifts are alive and active in Christ's Church, people may settle into an intellectual faith without the supernatural.***

The Holy Spirit Imperative

Unless the Revealing Gifts are alive and active in Christ's Church, people may settle into an intellectual faith without the supernatural.

The Spirit's "REVEALING" Gifts that Manifest God's Presence Are:

1. **The Word of Wisdom**. There are two aspects of this gift:

   1) God's Mysteries - He may reveal to you deep levels of understanding of God's mysteries (beyond human wisdom, reasoning, or formal training) concerning Christ, His Kingdom, and His purposes in the earth (1 Cor. 2:6-10).

   2) God's Solutions - The Word of Wisdom may also reveal the wisdom of God's solutions to humanly impossible dilemmas in life. This wisdom is beyond human reasoning. It's from God, who opens the spirit and mind of the gifted person to the wisdom of His mind.

2. **The Word of Knowledge**. There are two aspects as well:

   1) Knowledge of Scriptures - He may reveal to you deeper knowledge of scriptures beyond an ordinary Bible Study. It's the Holy Spirit "connecting the spiritual dots" for you to declare God's truth beyond your natural ability or education.

   2) Personal Matters - The Word of Knowledge may reveal to you hidden desires, upcoming events, or needs in a person that are unknown by you. This can also include warnings and declarations of God's purpose for them and His kind intentions for their lives. They are encouraging words from God bringing hope and confidence that God is with them. They are impressions from the Lord that He places in your heart and spirit concerning another person's life.

3. **The Distinguishing Between Spirits**. He may reveal whether spiritual activities are the workings of human spirits,

angelic spirits, or demonic spirits. It's impossible for a human being to discern between spirits, but the Holy Spirit can! **Human Spirits** are deeper than the soul or DNA of humankind. They comprise the root of all human inner natures, feelings, and motivations...even dominate human dispositions. *(E.g., a person's spirit can be haughty or jealous, or gentle and quiet. But with regeneration, fallen dispositions can be corrected.)* Human spirits live forever, even though the body dies. **Angelic Spirits** are God's ministering angels sent out by Him to serve, care for, protect and even warn His people. They have no bodies; however, they may take on human appearances for ministry purposes as directed by God. **Demonic Spirits** are Satan's evil angels that were cast out of heaven along with their master, the devil. They oppose God and His work through people on earth. Their evil assignment is to corrupt sound doctrine of the Gospel. In this way, they can deceive people into believing lies concerning Christ and His saving grace. They feed on and agitate the fallen natures of people to promote evil in the world. However, at the return of Christ, they will be judged by God through the witness of the redeemed, whom Christ has rescued from the devil's dark domain. And they will be cast into eternal torment in Hell...along with all who reject the saving grace of the Lord Jesus. ***Again, only through this Revealing Gift of the Holy Spirit can the distinguishing of these spirits be made.***

2) THE HOLY SPIRIT'S "SPEAKING" GIFTS

Across the years, we've attended many church services and ministry settings where the gifts of the Holy Spirit were flowing. We've also received prophetic words over our children, grandchildren, Sheila and me. Even before our grandchildren were born, God declared His righteous destiny and kind intentions for them. He's confirmed the future ministries that would flow through our children and grandchildren. And He's spoken things years ago that are now coming to pass. Even now, we see God's prophetic words manifesting while our grandchildren are still youths. A word from God settles all things. A word from God has set our family on a path of being a blessing to all who the Lord leads us to. Prophecies can even give us God's spiritual "strategies" for our lives (1 Tim. 1:18). Prophetic words are one of the many ways He loves us, cares for us, and makes our paths straight.

God really does speak to and through people in today's world, both corporately and individually. But many Christians **NEED A SIGN** (an attesting event) that God can interact and communicate with them directly and personally. Without questions, the highest revelation of God's "voice" is His written word, the Christian Bible. In fact, He's always speaking! He can speak through gifted Christians, pastors, and counselors. At times, He can even speak through life's situations. However, whenever God speaks through people, He will never violate or contradict His written word. If a person believes the Holy Spirit has spoken through or to them, it must always be judged by seasoned eldership in the Body of Christ who use the Holy Scriptures as God's Standard for evaluating what has been said. ***Unless the Speaking Gifts are alive and active in Christ's Church, people may believe that God is only an historical deity who remains silent and uninvolved in human lives.***

> **The Holy Spirit Imperative**
>
> **Unless the Speaking Gifts are alive and active in Christ's Church, people may believe God is only an historical deity who remains silent and uninvolved in human lives.**

The Spirit's "SPEAKING" Gifts that Manifest God's Presence Are:

1. **Prophecy.** There are two aspects of prophecy:

   1) Prophecy of Scripture - The apostle Peter declared that Scripture, in itself, is prophecy. It is God's word spoken through men who were moved on by the Holy Spirit (2 Pet. 1:20-21). This is the highest form of prophecy by which all other prophecies are judged.

   2) Prophecy to an Individual, Church or Nation - The Holy Spirit's gift of prophecy is one of the many ways that God speaks (communicates) with us personally or collectively. Prophecies are inspired messages from God to His people. Through prophetic words, God encourages, strengthens, builds up faith, comforts, confirms His will, and even warns people of impending dangers. Prophecies can speak to the past, the present, or things yet to come in human lives or in the world. Like all the other gifts of the Spirit, prophecies are given for the common good of all. A prophetic word is not a word-for-word "dictation" from God to the gifted person. Neither are they His verbal words spoken into human ears. They are divine impressions placed in the spirit and heart of the gifted person. They speak what they are sensing from God.

   (For much more extensive and deeper understandings of the gift of prophecy, I encourage you to read books written by Bishop Kirby Clements, who consistently walks in the office of a prophet.)

2. **Kinds of Tongues.** There are three aspects of this gift:

   1) Unlearned Languages - As on the day of Pentecost, God can gift a person to speak unlearned languages to people in their own native language (Acts 2:4-11). These are God's signs to the nations of His presence among them.

2) Prophetic Messages - At times, a prophetic message to a church may be declared in a public assembly by the spiritual language of tongues. However, if this is a valid message from the Lord, it must be interpreted by one who has the gift of Interpretation of Tongues (1 Cor. 14:5).

3) Personal Prayer Language - Many times we don't know what or how to pray for someone or a situation. Paul, who spoke in tongues more than most (1 Cor. 14:18), gave us insight. There is an aspect of tongues in which our spirit prays to God in mysteries, though our mind is unfruitful (1 Cor. 14:14). The Holy Spirit knows our weakness and intercedes for us through our utterances that transcend our rational intellect and understanding (Rom. 8:26). Praying in the Holy Spirit builds up our faith (1 Cor. 14:2-4). One additional benefit to praying in our prayer language is that it brings us into God's presence. In His presence, He brings us into alignment with His righteous intentions.

3. The Interpretation of Tongues. As mentioned above, a prophetic message in tongues to the church must be interpreted if the church is to be edified (1 Cor. 14:5). This interpretation is not like translating a known language into another known language (i.e., Spanish to English or English to Spanish). Like the Word of Knowledge and Prophecy, Interpretation of Tongues is an inner sense within the gifted person of what the Lord is speaking to His church. ***Again, as with all the Gifts of the Holy Spirit, they must be judged by God's written word, the ultimate prophecy to His people.***

3) THE HOLY SPIRIT'S "POWER" GIFTS

As many of you may know, I have been associated with the International Communion of Charismatic Churches since the middle 1980s and I've been teaching in the ICCC conferences since 2000. Most recently, I've been working even closer with the ministries of the ICCC. One of our colleagues, Bishop LaDonna Osborn, has a worldwide evangelistic and teaching ministry to the nations. Recently, I've seen videos of the Holy Spirit's power falling on many as she ministered God's healing grace and His love for them. It was literally breathtaking to watch blind eyes see, deaf ears hear, and the crippled walk again. This is one of the Holy Spirit's three Power Gifts in action. All these gifts are signs that point to God as the Creator of heaven and earth. When people experience His power manifested in their lives, they'll know that the Good News (the Gospel) of God's Kingdom and His redemptive grace has come among them. The amazement of God's Power Gifts confirms His supernatural presence and opens hearts to embrace the Savior.

God dwells in Heaven and Heaven is the dimension of His majesty and glory. It has no beginning, no end, and no passing of time. It is forever in the present. This is an entirely different spiritual dimension than our time-space world that He created for us. God is **omni-present** (spiritually present in heaven and earth at the same instant), **omniscient** (infinite knowledge and wisdom), **omnipotent** (infinite power to do whatever He so desires), and **omni-glorious** (the radiance of His splendor and majesty fills heaven and earth). Because He sees the past, present, and future with equal clarity, at His timing and discretion, He can "step" out of eternity into our world and our personal lives. This is when the supernatural meets the natural. He transcends both time and space. He transcends natural laws that govern our world and human existence (i.e., gravity, natural elements, illnesses, the anatomy of the human body, life, and death). His supernatural involvement with our world, and with you personally, isn't a "violation" of His creation; it is a sign that He is God and there is no other like Him. ***Unless the Power Gifts are alive and active in Christ's Church, people may discount the supernatural reality of the Christian Faith. Without the supernatural, Christianity is just another human philosophy.***

> The Holy Spirit Imperative
>
> **Unless the Power Gifts are alive and active in Christ's Church, people may discount the supernatural reality of the Christian Faith. Without the supernatural, Christianity is just another human philosophy.**

The Spirit's "POWER" Gifts that Manifest God's Presence Are:

1. **Faith.** This dimension of faith is different from the faith that all people must have if they are to receive Christ's saving grace. Through their human belief (faith) in the Gospel, they are born again. However, the faith of 1 Cor. 12:9 is a special impartation, not just a doctrinal belief. ***The Holy Spirit's Gift of Faith heads up the other Power Gifts, for without it, healings and miracles could never take place.*** This is an extraordinary faith that believes God for His supernatural and miraculous intervention, even in humanly impossible situations. This was the faith that Peter was filled with when he proclaimed the power of Jesus to heal the lame man (Acts 3:2-10). Whether the woman with an incurable hemorrhage had the Gift of Faith or not, her "desperate" faith touched God's heart, and healing power was released through Jesus (Mark 5:25-34).

2. **Gifts of Healings.** These gifts demonstrate the power of the Holy Spirit's anointing through believers to make people whole, cure diseases, and restore spiritual brokenness (Luke 4:18-19). Since the biblical words, "gifts" and "healings," are both plural, they indicate the power of God to heal more than one type of infirmity. God's supernatural healings repair and restore damaged or ailing human bodies. In His deep compassion for hurting people, He can make existing organs or limbs whole again. But this is not necessarily a "creative miracle," though physical healing can occur in that manner. This was the gift that Peter had when he healed Aeneas' paralytic body (Acts 9:33-34). ***It's important to know that God can heal anyway He desires. He can heal miraculously, progressively, or even by using the natural elements of the earth (Is. 38:1, 21; Mark 8:21-25; John 9:1-7).*** This means that God, at His discretion, may choose to add His supernatural healing grace to modern medicines. He can also give His wisdom to physicians to know what **to do** or what **not to do** to bring about healing. One final statement about divine healing: it can stand the test of physicians. If you believe God has healed you, make an appointment with your doctor to confirm it. This is what Jesus told the lepers to do after He healed them (Luke 5:12-14). This is a testimony to medical science that God can heal ailing bodies.

3. **Working of Miracles.** This is literally translated, "working of power." It's the sovereign working of God's power that transcends time and space to alter physical objects or change impossible situations. ***Miracles Are Not Necessarily Progressive in Action; They Are Instantaneous.*** Miracles have been and can be brought about in many ways:

- ***Changing Water to Wine* by Jesus was an obvious instant miracle (John 2:1-11).** It's important to understand that miracles are not for personal grandstanding. Jesus performed miracles as signs to reveal God's glory, and for people to put their trust in Him as the Savior. Gifts of Healings, as mentioned above, involve the restoring of existing organs or limbs.

- ***Instantaneous Healing can take place through Creative Miracles.*** An example of this is when Jesus gave eyesight to a man who was born blind. Jesus used wet soil (the dust of the earth that God used to create Adam) to reconstruct the man's eyes (John 9:1-7).

- ***Instantaneous Miracles can also bring a Dead Person Back to Life Again.*** This was the gift Peter had when he raised Tabitha from the dead (Acts 9:36-42). This was also the gift that Paul had when he raised Eutychus from the dead at Troas (Acts 20:9-10). Most definitely, the resurrection of Jesus from the dead was by the power of the Holy Spirit (Rom. 8:11). This same power that raised Him from the dead will resurrect us from the dead when we die in Christ (1 Thess. 4:14-17).

> The Holy Spirit Imperative
>
> **Again, without the manifestations of the Holy Spirit in a worship service, there is the missing dynamic of the supernatural working of God.**

Finally, and it bears repeating, without the manifestations of the Holy Spirit in a worship service, there is the missing dynamic of the supernatural working of God.

On a Personal Note Concerning the Gifts of the Holy Spirit, It's Important for Me to Make the Following Observations:

1. When people have the gifts of the Spirit confirmed in their lives, they activate them by faith, ***knowing God's kind and loving intentions for people.*** God never puts people on guilt trips. His Spirit leads us (never drives us) in the way of righteousness. If He corrects us (changes our course), it's so that we may share in His holiness (Heb. 12:10).

2. By no means can an ungifted person presumptuously "force" God to do anything by "putting a demand" on His power (Acts 19:13-16). That's called manipulation. ***God will never respond to anyone who tries to force His hand, regardless of who they are!***

3. All the gifts of the Holy Spirit are distributed to people just as He wills, not as we want (1 Cor. 12:11). And none of us have all these gifts, although every Christian has at least one (1 Cor. 12:7, 11). ***This means we need the gifts of God in one another (1 Cor. 12:27-31).*** This is how the church is edified.

4. The Gifts of the Holy Spirit are not about <u>**us**</u> who are gifted. They're about <u>**God**</u> and His grace working through us! We cannot supernaturally heal anyone by our own human abilities. And we dare not walk in pride believing we are more gifted than others. ***It's all about God and His people.*** He loves <u>**them**</u> so much, that he blesses them with His gifts in us. We are just human vessels He uses to supernaturally help and bless others.

5. The Gifts of the Holy Spirit to perform signs and wonders are distributed to every Christian (Mark 16:17-18). ***You don't have to be a leader in the church or a famous preacher.*** In fact, it may be a more impactful testimony of God's power for the gifts to flow through everyday Christians.

6. All the Gifts of the Holy Spirit are activated by faith. But so is everything else we need from God. As mentioned in the Gift of Faith on page 34, God can heal those who, by faith, cry out to Him for help. ***We serve a God who is merciful and moved with compassion to help a suffering world (Matt. 14:14).***

7. Finally, because God is sovereign, He can do anything He righteously wills to do, regardless of faith! He may choose to heal an unbeliever, just out of His mercy and compassion, so that the works of God can be displayed. Jesus did this for the blind man who didn't know who He was until after he was healed (John 9:25, 35-38). God did this for Naaman, commander of the Syrian army (enemies of God's people), even in his resistance (2 Kings 5:9-14). ***The reality is, faith or no faith, none of us deserve God's love, mercy, kindness, or healing. Remember, Jesus died for us even before we believed and while we were still in sin (Rom. 5:6-8).***

THE MINISTRY "GRACE-GIFTS" OF THE HOLY SPIRIT THROUGH YOU

Years ago, a young man in my pastoral group came to me with a question. *"I want to become more involved in our church,"* he began. *"But I don't know where to start. I don't even know what my gifts are. Can you help me?"* This wasn't an unusual request; I had spoken to many across the years who were looking for these same answers. The young man continued, *"I've read about the spiritual gifts of the Holy Spirit in 1 Corinthians 12, but these are way out of my league. I don't want to try to prophesy over people or perform miracles. I just what to be useful. I'm at a loss to know who I am and what God wants me to do. Can you help me?"* When I saw the honesty of his heart, I asked him to open his Bible and begin reading **Romans 12:1-8**. After an open discussion, I explained what this passage means and how it can be applied to his life. Afterwards, his eyes brightened as he said, *"Okay, think I know where to begin."*

We often speak of "Charismatic" Christians as those who operate in the supernatural gifts of 1 Corinthians 12:1-11. However, the word "Charismatic" is literally derived from the Greek word, "Charis," meaning "Grace!" Grace is God's freely given gift to His people. This can be empowerment unto salvation (Eph. 2:8), or it can be supernatural strength for endurance during suffering (2 Cor. 12:7-10). In fact, the Romans 12:1-8 gifts I shared with the young man, are also given by grace (Rom. 12:6). All gifts are given by the grace of God and are empowered by the Holy Spirit. ***(Though the Holy Spirit isn't mentioned in the Romans 12 gifts, He is the "Resident" God on earth who activates the will of the Father and the Son in our lives.)*** The apostle Peter encouraged the early Christians by telling them, ***"Each one** has received a special gift,* *employ it in serving one another as good stewards of the manifold grace of God"* (1 Pet. 4:10). All the different gifts we receive are needed to build up the Body of Christ. One gift is not more important than the others; they are different. ***Without the Romans 12:1-8 gifts of the Holy Spirit, the work and ministry of the church could not fulfill its mission on earth.*** The Bible doesn't tell us that God calls Apostles, Prophets, Evangelists, Pastors and Teachers to do ALL the ministry of the church. He calls them to equip (train and prepare) **THE SAINTS** (believers) for the work of the ministry and for the building up of the Body of Christ (Eph. 4:11-12)!

> The Holy Spirit Imperative
>
> Without the Romans 12:1-8 gifts of the Holy Spirit, the work and ministry of the church could not fulfill its mission on earth.

So, these questions must still be answered: **1) What are the Romans 12:1-8 gifts? 2) How do we receive them? 3) And how can we discover which gifts we have?** The reality is that every human being is born with natural talents and gifts. Some are skilled musicians and vocalists, some are eloquent speakers, some are leaders, some are administrators, some care for the hurting, and others fulfill needs in society. People can use their natural gifts for many reasons: personal gain, fame, even evil purposes, or for the good of society. ***But, for natural gifts to become used spiritually for the glory of God, it requires a supernatural transformation that renews the mind (Rom. 12:1-2).*** This is God's grace at work through the Holy Spirit. However, just as with all the gifts of the Spirit, they must be activated by the person's Christian faith that accepts and uses their gifts for God's glory (Rom. 12:3). The Ministry Grace-Gifts are recorded by the apostle Paul in his letter to the Roman church. Though these gifts have natural counterparts in each of us whether we're born again or not, God's grace transforms us and elevates our gifts to bring glory to His name.

1. **Prophecy**. Many believe this may be the same gift as the Office of the Prophet has in 1 Corinthians 12:10. However, some consider the preaching and teaching of God's word with divine authority (the prophecy of Scripture), as being prophetic. We proclaim God's word to people and draw them out of darkness into God's light. Through our gift, we strengthen, encourage, and comfort people (1 Cor. 14:3). ***Without this gift active in the church, we would have no preachers to proclaim God's heart and mind to people!***

2. **Service**. Regardless of your position in a local church, to serve means you do whatever is needed to promote the work of Christ's church, both locally and around the world. Christian service can speak to the **general work** of all who are called to serve Christ (Col. 3:23-24). Even the apostle Paul considered his work to be in the service of the Lord (1 Tim. 1:12). Service can also speak to the **Office of the Deacon** that carries out directives and serves the needs of believers (Acts 6:1-7). In 1 Corinthians 12:28, Paul lists **"Helps"** as those who serve by taking hold of whatever is needed to give aid and help. ***Without the Gift of Service active in the church, the work of Christ's Church would "grind to a halt" and never accomplish the will of God.***

3. **Teaching**. Again, many believe this may be the same gift as the Office of the Teacher in Ephesians 4:11. However, the gift of teaching may also include all Christians who have skills in explaining and imparting biblical and spiritual truth to others. These can be other church leaders (1 Tim. 3:2),

Bible Schools professors, and volunteers who conduct Bible classes or children's ministries in the church. ***Without this Teaching Gift active in the church, Christians would not have deeper understandings of God, His Church, and how to navigate life in Christ.***

4. **Exhortation.** There are many shades of meaning in this one word. It can mean consoling, comforting, encouraging, entreating, strengthening, instructing, and even warning people you care about. Exhortation isn't something you do from a distance. It speaks of walking beside someone and compassionately talking with them. It has authority, but it's also empathetic, feeling what a person is going through and reaching out to help them. ***Without this essential gift actively working in Christians, hurting people would not feel the love and comfort of God in their times of need.***

5. **Giving.** The heart of giving is generosity. It's freely giving from an open and willing heart, never out of a sense of obligation or reluctancy. Giving can be expressed by freely giving your money, time, personal skills, and provisions to contribute to the needs of others. It's imparting and sharing your resources without regret. This is a person who gives tithes and offerings to promote the work of their local church. They freely volunteer on church workdays and ministry outreach programs. And they use their other spiritual gifts to help the hurting. ***Without the Gift of Giving actively at work in a local church, God's resources that He has imparted to others will never benefit His Church.***

6. **Leading.** Leadership in God's Kingdom is different than we often see in the world. The Holy Spirit's Gift of Leading

involves the human authority of governing, but it's never dictatorial of authoritarian. It leads by example, not demand. It patterns itself after the leadership in the Good Shepherd, gentle and humble. Leaders guide and lead the way by virtue of their experiential wisdom. Leaders in Christ's church include all five Equipping Gifts of Eph. 4:11, Elders, Deacons, Youth Leaders and other Ministry Leaders. In 1 Corinthians 12:28, the apostle Paul speaks about Gifts of Administrations. This is the governing ***(steering)*** aspect of leadership. It directs an organization so that it reaches an intended outcome. Administrators are like ***helmsmen*** of ships; they steer the ship to arrive at the destination set by the captain. ***Without the Holy Spirit's Gift of Leading resident in a local church, the mission of the church and all its ministries and programs would stagnate with inactivity.***

7. **Mercy.** The Gift of Mercy is grounded in, and reflects, the very heart of God Himself. Just as He compassionately understands the frailty of humanity and its hopeless condition, so must we (Ps. 103:8-14). Mercy is God's gift to compassionately care for the hurting and disadvantaged of the world, regardless of their failures. Extending mercy to the afflicted is never an obligation or compulsion for those who have this gift; it readily flows out of their hearts. **However, mercy must also be tempered with wisdom and discernment.** If not, manipulating people may take advantage of your mercy to fulfill their devious purposes. This is why all the gifts of the Holy Spirit must work with discernment to represent God's righteous intentions. ***Without the Holy Spirit's Gift of Mercy alive in Christ's Church, we could never accurately represent His love and compassion to a hurting world.***

THE HOLY SPIRIT IS GOD'S "EMPOWERMENT" IN AND TROUGH YOU

When I was in seminary, one of the required courses offered was "Personal Evangelism." And as expected, the scriptural themes were Acts 1:8 ***(Power to be Christ's Witnesses),*** and Matthew 28:19-20 ***(Making Disciples).*** One of our assignments was to hand out tracts to unsuspecting bystanders, warning them of the horrors of Hell if they don't turn to Jesus. Another assignment was to find someone who was in a false religion and try to convert them to Christianity. I received an "A" in the course, but I failed miserably to be a witness or to make disciples. The whole experience left me empty and uncomfortable...and searching for answers. ***Years later in my pastoral ministry, this is what I discovered:***

- **Holy Spirit Empowerment Is "Dynamic!"** "Dunamis" is the Greek word for God's Power, which is where we derive the English word, "Dynamite" and "Dynamic." This means God's Empowerment is constant activity to bring about change. This speaks of God's power working within us to accomplish His will beyond our natural abilities (Eph. 3:20). ***When we are filled by the dynamic energy of God, He can do anything through us!***

- **The Holy Spirit Empowers You with HIS Gifts.** We previously covered all His gifts in detail on pages 25-43. Unless these are active in your life and local church, there is the missing dynamic of the supernatural working of God and His ministry gifts to serve others.

- **The Holy Spirit Empowers You with Courage, Boldness, and Confidence.** Because they had been filled with the Holy

Spirit, the Disciples were able to speak strongly against the rulers and elders who had crucified Jesus (Acts 4:8-14). Without courage, boldness, and confidence to step out of your comfort zone, it's impossible to be a witness for Christ.

- **The Holy Spirit Empowers Your Words with Conviction.** This is the only way a sinner can have his heart pierced with godly sorrow over his sins and turn to the Lord with repentance (Acts 2:37; 2 Cor. 7:10). If we can talk someone into trusting in Christ, someone else can talk them out of it. We may be able to give stirring speeches, but only the Holy Spirit can bring true conviction (John 16:8). ***Without the Holy Spirit's convicting power, we just become good motivational speakers!*** But also, the Holy Spirit can empower your gentle conversations, casual interactions, and unspoken influences to accomplish His work. You don't have to be a fiery evangelist or a powerful preacher to win people to Christ.

- **The Holy Spirit Empowers You to Be a Witness for Christ in the World.** This is immensely deeper than merely handing out fearful tracts. A witness is one who personally tells of Christ's saving grace **and** demonstrates it with his or her life, regardless of the consequences. (The Greek word for "Witness" is the derivation of the English word "Martyr.") Our witness for Christ never causes "guilt-trips." We tell people of God's love for them and His gracious offer of new life in Christ. We share with them the "Good News" that, through their faith in Christ's atoning work for them, their sins will be forgiven, and they will have eternal life. One additional reality is the power of our witness in the world. ***The return of Christ to the earth and His judgement against evil is inseparable from our witness in the*** *world (Matt. 24:14).* This means that those who die with belligerent and unrepented rejection of Christ's gracious offer of salvation, will be judged accordingly!

- **The Holy Spirit Empowers You to Make Disciples of the Nations.** This is the "Great Commission" of Matthew 28:18-20. "Making Disciples," is not a suggested option; it's Christ's command. A disciple is a "learner" of Christ, His ways, and His redemptive grace. Jesus' command is to make disciples of all "Nations." The biblical word for "Nations" is "Ethnos" ...all Ethnic groups of people. This speaks directly to all races and cultures. In other words, true disciples of Christ are all one in Christ. The Holy Spirit's work in redemption bridges all racial, social standing and gender differences in the world (Gal. 3:27-28). There are no prejudices in Christ!

Finally, does everyone you share Christ with become a Christian? Probably not. But when the Holy Spirit empowers your witness, your words will be like "spiritual seeds" planted in their hearts. The seed of salvation can be watered and grow by anointed preaching and teaching as well as by the witnesses of others (1 Cor. 3:6-7). Though you may not see instant results from your witness, more will come to Christ than if you had never shared Christ with them at all. ***Without the Holy Spirit's empowerment working through you, your ministry to others will just be human attempts to persuade, which will never bear the fruit of righteousness.***

The Holy Spirit Imperative

Without the Holy Spirit's empowerment working through you, your ministry to others will just be human attempts to persuade, which will never bear the fruit of righteousness.

THE "FRUIT" OF THE HOLY SPIRIT IN AND THROUGH YOU

I recall a parishioner speaking with me about how grateful he was to be filled with the Holy Spirit. When I asked him how he knew he was filled with the Spirit, he quickly responded, *"Well obviously; it's because I have the gift of speaking in tongues, just like the disciples on the Day of Pentecost!"* Knowing that he was a young Christian, I gave him a loving reality check. I began by confirming that it's a glorious blessing to be gifted by the Holy Spirit. Then I continued, ***"But do others see His 'Christ-Forming Grace' demonstrated through your life?"*** With a puzzled look on his face he asked, *"What's that?"* I asked him to open his Bible to Galatians 5:13-26. Then I took some time to help him understand the Fruit of the Spirit and how others recognize that Christ actually lives in him. ***I concluded our discussion by revealing that when people see these righteous virtues demonstrated through his life, they will know for sure that he has been "Filled" with God's Spirit.***

All of us as Christians are in a Spiritual Growth Process...even until the day we transition to heaven. God's Spirit is progressively conforming (fashioning) us into the image of Christ (Rom. 8:29). The more we yield to (live by) the Holy Spirit, the more we are cultivating Christ-like behavior. As such, we are in that glorious progression of being transformed into Christlikeness (Rom. 12:2).

It's important to note here that even as a believer, it's impossible for you to consistently produce the Fruit of Righteous Behavior. But when the Holy Spirit manifests His grace through you, others will recognize Christ in you. This is in stark contrast to the deeds of our sinful nature that Paul listed in Galatians 5:15-21.

The Fruit of the Spirit begins with "Love" and ends with "Self-Control." It's interesting that "Fruit" is a singular noun, meaning that all nine graces do not operate apart from the others. They are unified into one glorious manifestation.

1. **Love.** We promote the good of others even at our own expense. This is what Jesus did for us (2 Cor. 5:21).

2. Joy. We are independent of outward circumstances. We're filled with the inner joy of Christ and eternal life (1 Pet. 1:8-9).

3. **Peace**. We are quiet even in adversity. We know the Father is in control of our lives when we're not (John 14:27).

4. **Patience**. We're slow to anger when wronged. We reject trying to get even with others (2 Tim. 2:24).

5. **Kindness**. We're thoughtful and considerate toward people who provoke us. We always do good to them (Luke 6:35).

6. **Goodness**. With an upright and tender heart, we are humble, compassionate, and patient toward others (Col. 3:12).

7. **Faithfulness**. We are filled and established with faith toward God. We are always trustworthy and reliable (Luke 16:10–12).

8. **Gentleness**. We are mild and considerate toward others, never throwing our weight around (Titus 3:2 NLT).

9. **Self-control**. This is the most difficult of all. We refuse to be a slave to wrong desires and emotional reactions (Gal. 5:16).

However, when we read and consider these nine unified virtues of the Holy Spirit working through us, it's easy to fall into two traps:

- **Legalism** - Trying to gain God's favor and His love by our attempts to exhibit perfect conduct. It's easy to boast about sins we **don't** commit, while conveniently forgetting the ones we do commit. It's impossible to keep God's law (James 2:10)

- **Self-Condemnation** - This is a never-ending "guilt trip" every time we fail to live by the Spirit. Sooner or later we realize that our fallen nature will never live up to God's righteous expectation. That's why we need a Savior!

What, then, does the apostle Paul mean in Galatians 5:24, *"Those who belong to Christ Jesus have crucified the flesh with its passions and desires?"* It means we must also read Galatians 2:20, *"I **Have Been** crucified with Christ; and it is no longer I who live, but Christ lives in me; and the life which I now live in the flesh I live by faith in the Son of God, who loved me and gave Himself up for me."* When Jesus suffered the penalty of sin for us, He gave us **HIS** righteousness and its fruit (2 Cor. 5:21; Eph. 5:9). However, that does not release us from the responsibility of personal discipline, repenting (changing), seeking forgiveness, and living a forgiven life. ***Remember, without the Holy Spirit's Fruit expressed through our "clay vessels," the world will never know that these virtues are from Him and not from ourselves (2 Cor. 4:7)!***

> The Holy Spirit Imperative
>
> **Without the Holy Spirit's Fruit expressed through our "clay vessels," the world will never know that these virtues are from Him and not from ourselves!**

THE HOLY SPIRIT IS CHRIST'S "FRAGRANCE" IN AND TROUGH YOU

When my wife, Sheila, returned from a quick shopping trip to a craft store, she excitedly announced, *"I can't wait to tell you what happened at the store today!"* She shared with me about walking into a craft shop that she hadn't planned on visiting. (During those days, there had been difficult racial conflicts reported all over the news.) As she turned to walk down an aisle, she came face to face with a lovely African American lady she had never met before. When the lady gave her an unexpected compliment, Sheila thanked her and quietly said, *"What you have heard, felt and seen, I don't feel that way toward you at all."* Then Sheila asked, *"Would you mind if I gave you a hug?"* She nodded her head and as Sheila hugged her, the lady began to weep. Sensing that they were both Christians and that the Spirit of the Lord was present in them, Sheila began speaking prophetically over her life. Finally, Sheila told her, *"I believe in divine appointments, and this has been definitely set up by the Lord for both of us."* This was one of many occasions where people sensed the Spirit of God in Sheila and that she sensed He was in them as well.

Paul's passage in **2 Cor. 2:14–16** can be difficult to understand. He speaks of *"Christ manifesting through us the* ***Sweet Aroma*** *of the knowledge of Him in every place."* He continues by revealing that *"We are a* ***Fragrance of Christ*** *to God among those who are being saved and among those who are perishing."* Then he gives us an even more specific description of this fragrance: *"To the one an aroma from* ***Death to Death****, to the other an aroma from* ***Life to Life****!"* What, then, can this possibly mean?

God doesn't have a natural sense of smell, but just as a sweet aroma is soothing to us, so are we to God. We, who have been redeemed by the sacrificial death of His Son, are like a soothing aroma to our Lord. Not only does God sense the "fragrance" of spiritual redemption, but so do we. We sense spiritual life in others who are on the way of salvation, and they sense it in us (2 Cor. 2:15 Message Bible). ***Could this be a foretaste of heaven? The fulness of all the glories of heaven are indescribable. But most certainly, the knowledge of the Savior, who gave us His victory over sin and death, will be like a sweet fragrance diffused throughout our heavenly abode!***

Also, it's not as if we can physically "smell" something in the spiritual realm, but we have a spiritual sense of awareness (perception) of it. This means we can spiritually sense if a person has the eternal life of Christ dwelling in them or not. And for those who are perishing, we sense the stench of spiritual death. Not only that, but those who are hardened in unbelief without any intention of repentance, may even despise or war against Christ in us.

There is a book of the Bible that some may question how it ever came to be included as a "holy book" in our canon of scripture. It's the Song of Solomon (Song of Songs). When taken literally, it's a provocative (and sensual) story of love expressed between Solomon and his favorite wife. To others, it's just a poem extolling human love and the freedom of communication of that love. But to us, who are the redeemed, it's a portrait of the great love between Christ and His Church. The King represents Jesus and the Bride represents His redeemed people. In the Song of Solomon, we learn that the interaction between Christ and us speaks of both His and our "fragrances" (Song 1:2-3, 12-14). It recounts the beckoning of the King for His bride to "come away" with Him to a secret place (Song 2:10-14). And it speaks of Christ being captivated by our beauty (Song 1:15; 4:7; 7:5-6).

> **The Holy Spirit Imperative**
>
> **Without His fragrance present in our lives and in the lives of others, we may not have this glorious foretaste of heaven.**

I know this is difficult to understand in light of our sinful natures, but God really does love us, and His desire is for us! He loves all people, regardless of their lostness. That's why He came to earth, took on flesh, showed us who the Father really is, and redeemed us back to Him (John 14:8-9; John 3:16). We, who are redeemed, are a sweet aroma to Him, and He is to us. ***The Holy Spirit is the One who produces this divine fragrance. Without His fragrance present in our lives and in the lives of others, we may not have this glorious foretaste of heaven.***

V - The Power and Ministry of the Holy Spirit in Christ's Church

I recall, as if it were just yesterday, when Sheila and I first experienced the real Presence of the Holy Spirit in our hearts. It was in the early 1970s when the Charismatic Movement was spreading through historical churches. Someone had given us a cassette tape recording of an outdoor worship service. Amazing worship! The pastor was worshiping God in the Spirit with free-flowing music, prophetic songs, and gentle words of God's love and presence flowing from his heart. Coming from a Presbyterian background, this kind of freedom in worship was exhilarating. I was used to trained choirs and sermons from scripts. I was captivated! Those were also the glorious days when I first sensed the Lord's call to shepherd the flock of God for the rest of my life.

WHAT WOULD THE CHURCH BE...WITHOUT THE HOLY SPIRIT?

What makes Christianity different from all other religions and philosophies of the world? It's the supernatural Presence of the Holy Spirit! He reveals the eternal reality of the Living God and His personal love for all people. All writings of world religions and ideologies contain moral and philosophical truth. But only in Christianity do you find Redemptive Truth. Redemptive Truth is the reality that God loves fallen humanity so much that He came to the earth to rescue us from all that would ruin our souls, both now and in eternity. *Without the Holy Spirit's work in Christ's*

Church, His life, death, and resurrection for the forgiveness of our sins would be just a concept rather than reality.

What else would the church be like without the power and ministry of the Holy Spirit? I'll recount for you the **"Holy Spirit Imperative"** points I emphasized in the previous chapters of this book.

1. Without the **"Manifestations of the Holy Spirit"** in a worship service, there is the missing dynamic of the supernatural working of God. (Pages 25-26)

2. Unless the Holy Spirit's **"Revealing Gifts"** are alive and active in Christ's Church, people may settle into an intellectual faith without the supernatural. (Pages 26-29)

3. Unless the Holy Spirit's **"Speaking Gifts"** are alive and active in Christ's Church, people may believe God is only an historical deity who remains silent and uninvolved in human lives. (Pages 29-32)

4. Unless the Holy Spirit's **"Power Gifts"** are alive and active in Christ's Church, people may discount the supernatural reality of the Christian Faith. Without the supernatural, Christianity is just another human philosophy. (Pages 33-38)

5. Without the Romans 12:1-8 **"Ministry Grace-Gifts"** of the Holy Spirit, the work and ministry of the church could not fulfill its mission on earth. (Pages 39-40)

6. Without the Holy Spirit's **"Gift of Prophecy"** active in the church, we would have no preachers to proclaim God's heart and mind to people! (Page 41)

7. Without the Holy Spirit's **"Gift of Service"** active in the church, the work of Christ's Church would "grind to a halt" and never accomplish the will of God. (Page 41)

8. Without the Holy Spirit's **"Teaching Gift"** active in the church, Christians would not have deeper understandings of God, His Church, and how to navigate life in Christ. (Page 41)

9. Without the Holy Spirit's **"Gift of Exhortation"** actively working in Christians, hurting people would not feel the love and comfort of God in their times of need. (Page 42)

10. Without the Holy Spirit's **"Gift of Giving"** actively at work in a local church, God's resources that He has imparted to others will never benefit His Church. (Page 42)

11. Without the Holy Spirit's **"Gift of Leading"** resident in a local church, the mission of the church and all its ministries and programs would stagnate with inactivity. (Pages 42-43)

12. Without the Holy Spirit's **"Gift of Mercy"** alive in Christ's Church, we could never accurately represent Christ's love and compassion to a hurting world. (Page 43)

LEADERSHIP IN CHRIST'S CHURCH... WITHOUT THE HOLY SPIRIT

Unfortunately, we would just be good motivational speakers and social activates! We would only be human leaders with personal agendas, some good and others self-serving. Without the anointing of the Holy Spirit, we could not be chosen instruments through whom the Holy Spirit brings redemptive truth and transforms lives into the glorious spiritual "image" of Christ (2 Cor. 3:18). This only happens through a spiritual metamorphosis that begins on the inside by the New Birth and produces an outward character and nature that reflects Christ. Gifted orators may stir the emotions and inspire people to action. But Christ's Saving Grace can only be imparted by the Holy Spirit working through Preachers and Teachers of the Gospel (Rom. 10:13-17).

IS THERE A HIERARCHY OF GIFTS AND CALLINGS AMONG CHURCH LEADERS?

I was part of a church many years ago where the senior pastor defined the Five Equipping Gifts as headed up by the Apostles. Basically, they were at the top of the ecclesiastical "totem pole" and Teachers were at the bottom as the very least of the callings. *(As a called Teacher of God's word, you can imagine how that made me feel!)* As a proof-text, he used 1 Corinthians 12:28, "First Apostles, Second Prophets, and Third Teachers." It was difficult for me to harmonize this concept with Paul's analogy that all members of the human body are needed, and none is greater than others (1 Cor. 12:14-27). This stirred me to diligently study the Scriptures (specifically Eph. 4:11-16) to better understand God's

> The Holy Spirit Imperative
>
> **Especially in today's world, we need all Five Equipping Gifts, which are imparted by the Holy Spirit, to work in harmony for believers to "grow up" in spiritual maturity.**

intentions for His Church. This is how I came to understand that Paul was speaking of the **chronological order** of how Christ's Church was established. ***Especially in today's world, we need all Five Equipping Gifts, which are imparted by the Holy Spirit, to work in harmony for believers to "grow up" in spiritual maturity (Eph. 4:11-16).*** No one of us has all these gifts wrapped up in one person. We need one another for the edifying of the church and its growth in Christ. The Equipping Gifts in the Church are:

1. **Apostles.** Apostles appear "first" in the 1 Corinthians 12:28 passage only because the early church began when Christ sent them out with the message of the Gospel. They planted local churches and established sound doctrine. Modern day Apostles do not have the same authority as the foundational Apostles who were inspired to write Scripture. Nevertheless, today's Apostles are trans-local in their ministries sent out by Christ to plant and nurture churches. ***Without called Apostles, along with all other Ephesians 4:11 gifts, Christ's Church cannot fully accomplish its mission on earth.***

2. **Prophets.** Prophets are "second," not as in a hierarchy, but because they were also gifted men who founded Christ's Church (Eph. 2:20). They, along with Apostles, were inspired by the Holy Spirit to deliver the prophecy of Scripture, which has now become our Christian Bible (2 Pet. 1:20-21). Today's prophets do not write Scripture, but they continue to declare the heart and mind of God to His people. They strengthen, encourage, and comfort people with prophetic words that reveal hidden desires, upcoming events, or needs in a person's life. They can also bring warnings and declarations of God's purpose and kind intentions for people. They, along with other gifted men and women, are essential gifts in the

Body of Christ. ***And again, without called Prophets, along with all other Ephesians 4:11 gifts, Christ's Church cannot fully accomplish its mission on earth.***

3. **Evangelists.** Even the name, "Evangelist," (which is a Greek form of the word "Gospel") reveals who they are and their essential function in the Body of Christ. The evangelist heralds the "Good News" and "Glad Tidings" that God is among men and women to bring salvation to all who believe. They proclaim God's Kingdom of Righteousness that is available to all. They are sent out from the local church to preach the Gospel to the unsaved. They are soul winners, church planters and cultural transformers. Their ministries may certainly include praying for people to receive the Holy Spirit and performing signs and wonders. ***Again, without called Evangelists, along with all other Ephesians 4:11 gifts, Christ's Church cannot fully accomplish its mission on earth.***

4. **Pastors.** Pastors are under-shepherds of Christ, the Chief Shepherd. They care for the "flock" of God, which is the local congregation where they serve. They preach, teach, guard, and give guidance to God's people from His word. (This is why some view this gifting to be the "Pastor/Teacher," in which both gifts are given to the same individual.) They further explain the meanings of Scripture and give personal applications for God's people to follow. Their ministries may also include praying for people to receive the Holy Spirit and performing signs and wonders. ***One more time, without called Pastors, along with all other Ephesians 4:11 gifts, Christ's Church cannot fully accomplish its mission on earth.***

5. **Teachers.** It was not because Teachers were less important or less needed that they were named "third" in 1 Corinthians 12:28. It was because during the formation of the New Testament Church, they followed the Apostles and Prophets to bring clarity and understanding to young Christians in the early church. Today's teachers fulfill a similar role. They help establish the believer's faith by systematically explaining and imparting the truth, wisdom and understanding of God's word with practical applications for life (Col. 1:28). ***And finally, without called Teachers, along with all other Ephesians 4:11 gifts, Christ's Church cannot fully accomplish its mission on earth.***

A Concluding Statement:

Apostolic, Prophetic, Evangelistic, Pastoral and Teaching Gifts of Eph. 4:11 Are Not Limited to Church Leaders.

This statement may be a bit controversial for those who believe the Five Equipping Gifts are leadership gifts uniquely given only to the clergy. Certainly, these Five Equipping Gifts have gifted leaders among them. ***But look closely at how the apostle Paul introduced these gifts. The book of Ephesians was not written to church leaders; it was addressed to Christians in general.*** It's about gifts, not leaders. However, leading is most definitely one of the many Romans 12:1-8 gifts that God may add to a person's other gifts. Read again Paul's opening statement in Ephesians 4:7.

> *"But to **EACH ONE of Us** grace was given according to the measure of Christ's gift."*

In the church where I served for 30 years, I recognized these five giftings in congregational members who were not designated or considered to be leaders. They were strong Christians who loved the Lord and served with the gifts God gave them. Some were sent out as Apostolic teams with pastors to plant churches in other cities. Some spoke Prophetically during personal ministry to other Christians. Others had Evangelistic hearts to share the Gospel with unbelievers. Many, who had Shepherding hearts, assisted me with my pastoral duties. And still others with Teaching gifts accurately explained passages of scriptures to their friends and family. All these gifted men and women, without having leadership titles, were involved in "equipping" the saints (Eph. 4:12). ***The more we focus on serving with the Holy Spirit's gifts and less on leadership titles, the more Christ's Church will be built up and grow into maturity.***

> The Holy Spirit Imperative
>
> **The more we focus on serving with the Holy Spirit's gifts and less on leadership titles, the more Christ's Church will be built up and grow into maturity.**

THE HOLY SPIRIT AND THE BRIDE OF CHRIST

When we speak of the Power and Ministry of the Holy Spirit, we must never forget His work in preparing the church to become the glorious Bride of Christ. Using metaphorical language, the Bible portrays the love relationship between Christ and His Church as a loving Bridegroom and His cherished Bride. In human terms, a godly marriage is the union of a man and a woman in a holy covenant of love, trust, faithfulness, and mutual commitment throughout life. But this comparison is merely a shadow of how it will be at the culmination of the ages. God's redeemed people, cleansed from all the blemishes of our sins, will be eternally and inseparably joined to the Lord. *(What a Good God We Serve!)*

As mentioned on pages 51-52, the **Song of Solomon** is a portrait of the great love between Christ and His Church. The King represents Jesus and the Bride represents His redeemed people. In the book of **Hosea**, we see the prophetic story of the grace and forgiveness of God when He restores His "unfaithful wife" (His people who forsook Him) back to Himself. **Jesus** gave us deeper insight in His parable in Matthew 22:1-14 of the King (the Father) who prepared a wedding banquet for His Son (Jesus). But those who were not "clothed in Christ" (the redeemed) are forever excluded from the wedding. The true Bride of Christ can only be those who have responded to God's beckoning through the prophets and preachers of the Gospel. The **apostle Paul**, under the inspiration of the Holy Spirit, paints the picture even more clear with the spiritual comparison of husbands and wives in Ephesians 5:25-32. ***The Bride of Christ will be made clean, holy, and blameless, which is possible only through the Substitutionary Atonement of Jesus, which is applied by the Holy Spirit.***

In Revelation 19:7 and 21:2 the apostle John revealed dual truths: 1) The Church must ***"Make Herself Ready"*** by putting on Christ and doing the works of Jesus; (2) The Church has ***"Been Made Ready"*** by the sanctifying work of the Holy Spirit. Then, near the end of John's revelation, the Spirit made a startling revelation, *"Come here; I will show you the bride, the **Wife** of the Lamb"* (Rev. 21:9). Notice in this passage, we're no longer a New "Bride," we have become the Mature and Radiant "Wife" of Christ. ***This is not only what the Holy Spirit showed John about our future, it shows us who we should be NOW...even before Christ returns.***

1. We're trusted *to Share in God's Glory* (Rev. 21:11).

2. We're a *Righteous Light and Witness* in a world of darkness (Rev. 21:11).

3. We're founded on the revelation of both the *Old and New Testaments* (Rev. 21:12-14).

4. We're marked by *Equality, Justice, and Integrity* (Rev. 21:15-17).

5. We're the *Permanent Habitation* of God Himself (Rev. 21:22-23).

6. We're *Multi-Cultural*—all prejudice is gone (Rev. 21:24).

7. We're a *Community of Abundance* (Rev. 21:24-26).

8. We're a people *Redeemed and Restored* (Rev. 21:27).

Finally, look how John's final revelation in the Bible concludes:

> *"The Spirit and the Bride Say, 'Come.'" And let the one who hears say, "Come." And let the one who is thirsty come; let the one who wishes take the water of life without cost." - Rev. 22:17*

The Holy Spirit Imperative

Without the Holy Spirit working with us, our witness to the world would be fruitless.

As the Holy Spirit continues to prepare us to be the Bride of Christ, He joins with us to beckon a fallen world to partake of the Water of Life that only Christ can give (John 4:13-14). ***Without the Holy Spirit working with us, our witness to the world would be fruitless.***

VI - The Power and Ministry of the Holy Spirit in The Kingdom of God

When I first heard the message of the Kingdom of God, it connected all the "spiritual dots" in my studies of Scripture. It forever shaped and reshaped my ministry and teaching. I learned that the Kingdom of God is the present reality of God's righteous rule and dominion through the Lord Jesus in every sphere of existence in the universe. God is sovereign over all the kingdoms of the world and His Kingdom is forever. I also learned that the assignment of the redeemed is to demonstrate His Kingdom on earth as it is in heaven.

For the first time, I saw the overarching panorama of the history of the world and the culmination of the ages. God's eternal plan was "circular" rather than "linear." It will end as it began, with God's Kingdom of Righteousness, Peace and Joy. To illustrate this, I developed the following teaching diagram.

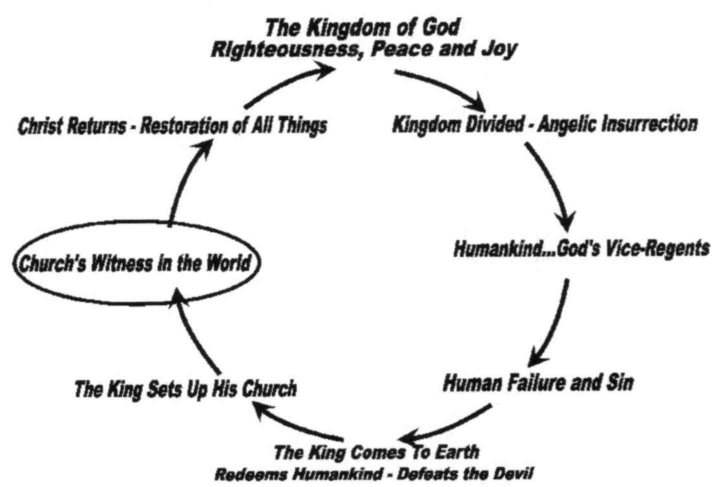

1. **The Kingdom of God – Righteousness, Peace and Joy.** In the beginning, before creation, there was God. His pre-sin creation of angels, humans, and animals, lived in a world of Righteousness, Peace, Harmony and Joy.

2. **The Kingdom Was Divided by an Angelic Insurrection.** Through freedom of choice, Lucifer and a third of the angels rebelled against God and were cast out of heaven. Thus, their evil kingdom of spiritual darkness came to the Earth.

3. **Humankind - God's Vice-Regents of the Earth.** When God created Adam and Eve, He gave them a strategic mission to rule over the earth with His character and integrity. Their assignment was to rule and take dominion over all creation with God and to "guard" (Hebrew definition of "keep") the Garden of Eden, which most certainly included ruling over any force that would oppose God's righteous purposes on earth.

4. **Human Failure and Sin.** To give Adam and Eve the first opportunity to fulfill their assignment of dominion and rule, God allowed Satan to appear in the form of a serpent in the Garden of Eden and challenge His authority. But they failed. They listened to Satan's deceptive words. Thus, sin became more than an act; it became part of all human nature.

5. **The King Came to the Earth, Redeemed Humanity, and Defeated Satan.** Even before sin entered the world, the Triune God determined that the Son would come to earth, take on human flesh, receive upon Himself the sin of the world and the punishment that humankind deserves, and give His righteousness ***to all who trust in His redemptive work.***

Jesus (God's Son) stood victorious against the devil's temptations and rendered him powerless over spiritual death ***for all who trust in Christ.*** Thus, the Second Person of the Triune God (the Son of God and King of God's Kingdom) fully accomplished all that Adam and Eve failed to do.

6. **The King Set Up His Church.** The Church that Jesus built is not a religious or legalistic hierarchy. It's founded on the King's New Covenant in which redemption was purchased by the sacrifice of the King Himself rather than the blood of bulls and goats. His Church is His people (not institutions), who have been "called out" of Satan's dark kingdom of sin and transferred into God's righteous Kingdom of Light. Jesus restored true spiritual authority to His followers and gave them dominion over Satan's evil influences, ***which was God's original intentions for Adam and Eve.***

7. **The Church's Witness in the World.** As the redeemed of the Lord, we personally tell of Christ's saving grace and demonstrate it with our own lives. The King sends us as Lights of His righteous Kingdom into the dark and evil kingdoms of the world to represent (witness to) the Light of His redemptive work. Those who accept our witness and turn to the Lord will be saved, but those who reject our witness will be condemned. Our witness is NOT our sinless lives (for our fallen nature is always with us). Rather it is our redeemed lives in which we willingly repent, ask for forgiveness and trust in the Lord Jesus Christ. Thus, our faith is an overcoming witness even against the devil...for he will never repent! ***The witness of Christ's Church in the world is so important that He will not return to the earth until that witness of His righteous Kingdom is complete.***

8. **Christ Will Return and Restore All Things to Righteousness, Peace and Joy.** At last, the Great Drama of God will be complete. God's universe will finally be brought full circle. That which existed before sin entered the world will be restored...but even greater! The earth, once corrupted and groaning from the consequences of sin, will be set free from its slavery, purged of evil and renewed into the dwelling place of God and His redeemed people (Rom. 8:18-23). We, who are the redeemed of the Lord, will be raised from the dead, receive glorified bodies, and shall join the King as co-rulers with Him on the earth. The devil, his angels, and all who followed him will receive the just punishment that is due to them...never again to trouble the earth. And the Lord Jesus Christ, the King of God's Kingdom, will hand over the kingdoms of the world to the Father that had been won by Him and His Victorious Church. And He shall receive glory and honor forever from the angels and all His redeemed people. ***His infinite grace, wisdom and love has been demonstrated by reversing evil and restoring His universe back to Righteousness, Joy, and Peace once again. Never again shall there be pain, suffering or death on the earth.***

The Holy Spirit Is Inseparable from the Kingdom of God

Within this great Drama of Good and Evil, the Holy Spirit is God's "Key Player." In fact, Scripture even defines the Kingdom of God as Righteousness, Peace and Joy IN THE HOLY SPIRIT (Rom. 14:17)! ***He was (and is) intrinsically involved in every aspect of God's Kingdom and His overarching plan for the world and the culmination of the ages.*** As mentioned before, these are some of the Holy Spirits works in God's Kingdom:

1. ***Together, God the Father, God the Son, and God the Holy Spirit exercise eternal dominion in the Kingdom of God, both in heaven and on earth!*** The Kingdom of God always was, always is, and always shall be. The Great Triune God eternally existed in holy communion, even before time began.

2. ***Without the Holy Spirit, the world wouldn't exist!*** The creation of the heavens and the earth were established by the full Triune God, Father, Son, and Holy Spirit. When God "spoke" the world into existence (waters, land, vegetation, animals, the sun, the moon and the stars), the power of the Holy Spirit accomplished what He spoke.

3. ***Without the Holy Spirit fulfilling God's spoken word to shine His Light into spiritual darkness and chaos, they could never have been overpowered!*** The power of the full Godhead cast Lucifer and his angels out of heaven to the earth. The Holy Spirit was the One who "hovered" over the spiritual darkness on the earth that had been corrupted by Satan's evil kingdom.

4. ***Without the Holy Spirit, the entire human race wouldn't exist!*** The Holy Spirit was there at the beginning of humankind. He was the "Breath" of God that breathed life into Adam's lifeless form and made him a living soul.

5. ***Without the Holy Spirit, we would not receive the general blessings of food, rain, and shelter even for unbelievers!*** The Holy Spirit was (and is) the power behind God's Common Grace. He originates, maintains, strengthens, and guides all life (organic, intellectual, and moral) toward God's ultimate purposes.

6. ***Were it not for the supernatural conception of Jesus by the Holy Spirit, we would not have a Savior who can sympathize with the weaknesses of humanity!*** For the Son of God to become flesh, born of a woman yet fully God, the Holy Spirit had to come upon Mary to bear the Holy Child.

7. ***Jesus could never have been empowered and anointed for His earthly ministry without the Holy Spirit!*** The Spirit "descended upon Him as a dove" at His baptism with a spoken confirmation from the Father (Matt. 3:16-17). Jesus was led by the Spirit to overcome Satan's temptation (Matt. 4:1-11). And Jesus was anointed by the Holy Spirit when He began His ministry on earth (Luke. 4:18-21).

8. ***Jesus could never have built His Church without the Holy Spirit!*** Jesus' Church is not an institution or building; it's His believers who are Born Again by the Spirit of God. Without Born Again believers, there would be no Church to be witnesses for Christ in the world.

9. ***Without the Holy Spirit, Jesus could never have been resurrected and we would still be dead in our sins!*** The resurrection of Jesus proved that He was victorious over the power of death (Acts 2:24; Rom. 8:11). Because He was victorious over sin and death, our faith is not worthless, and we can walk in newness of life (Rom. 6:4; 1 Cor. 15:14-17).

10. ***Without the supernatural power of the Holy Spirit, human strength alone can never overcome evil and Satan's power!*** By the power of the Holy Spirit, Jesus cast out demons, proving the authority of God's Kingdom over Satan's

wicked kingdom (Matt. 12:28). Jesus also gave us His authority and the power of the Spirit to cast out unclean spirits and heal every kind of disease (Matt. 10:1--8).

11. ***Without the power of the Holy Spirit, those who die in Christ could never be resurrected to eternal life!*** Death is one of the greatest fears that men and women face. What lies beyond death? Is it heaven, hell, or non-existence? For we who are the redeemed, there is no fear. Through the power of the Holy Spirit, we shall be raised and given bodies that never die (2 Cor. 4:14; John 5:28-29; Rev. 21:4).

12. ***Without the Holy Spirit, we wouldn't even know there is the Kingdom of God or what it is!*** When Jesus completed His earthly mission and returned to heaven, He sent the Holy Spirit to be with us and live in us. The Holy Spirit is the One who takes what Jesus has and reveals it to us (John 16:14). Since Jesus is the King of God's Kingdom, the Holy Spirit also reveals to us God's vast Kingdom. This is why the Apostle Paul wrote, **"The Kingdom of God Is Righteousness, Peace and Joy...In the Holy Spirit! (Rom. 14:17).**

THE HOLY SPIRIT IS THE "ADMINISTRATOR" OF GOD'S KINGDOM

In the church where I ministered for 30 years, I was assigned many responsibilities. Because of my pastoral heart and teaching gift, it was an honor to shepherd God's people and teach in our Bible School. Because of my education and experience in engineering, I sat on most of the administrative committees of the church. In my administrative duties, I was involved in strategic planning with the

Senior Pastor and his advisors. Then I, along with the pastoral staff, implemented our agreed upon directions for the church. I was humbled to be trusted to build and maintain church facilities, co-found our Bible School, develop and oversee committees, train pastors and church leaders, and equip the saints for the work of the ministry. These types of managerial activities are not unlike the administrative work of the Holy Spirit in the world.

The Kingdom of God is the past, present, and future reality of God's righteous rule and dominion in every sphere of existence in heaven and earth. The eternal plan of God's Kingdom (as described on pages 63-66) requires divine coordination and timing. Fulfilling God's purposes in His created universe is never left to chance or random events. Every appearance of God and His angels, every prophetic utterance, every fulfillment of prophecy, every miracle, every judgment, every blessing, every divine appointment, every evil that is turned into good, and everything that happens or doesn't happen in God's Kingdom, is overseen and managed by God.

However, this amazing spiritual reality never violates the freedom of human choice. Though God has infinite foreknowledge of all human decisions and actions, it doesn't mean that he foreordains them to happen beyond human will. People choose of their own free will to reject or accept God's love and redemptive grace, regardless of His righteous plan for their lives (Jer. 18:7-10).

Nevertheless, God's predetermined decrees are His unchangeable and irreversible mandates that will surely come to pass, regardless of human involvement or lack of involvement. Examples of His decrees can be found in Gen. 3:15; Num. 14:21; Ps. 33:11; Is. 46:9-11; Matt. 16:18-19; Heb. 6:17). ***Every aspect of God's eternal plan in His Kingdom that fulfills His intended end and brings glory to Him, is*** *executed and administrated by the Holy Spirit (Zech. 4:6; Matt. 4:1).* This is why He can be called the "Administrator" of God's Kingdom.

Using the analogy of earthly "administration" that is needed to conduct human affairs, we can draw a parallel to understand how the Holy Spirit works in God's overall plan for heaven and earth.

The Holy Spirit Imperative

Every aspect of God's eternal plan in His Kingdom that fulfills His intended end and brings glory to Him, is executed and administrated by the Holy Spirit.

How, Then, Does the Holy Spirit Administrate God's Kingdom?

Here Are a Few Examples:

1. **The Holy Spirit Was There in the Beginning.**
   A corporate administrator is personally involved in all planning processes from beginning to end. So was the Holy Spirit. ***God's strategy and eternal plan was determined by the counsel of the Father, the Son and the Holy Spirit working together before time began (Eph. 1:4-11; Rev. 13:8).***

2. **The Holy Spirit Leads, Guides and Directs the Lives of All Who Dwell in His Kingdom.**
   The role of an office administrator includes providing leadership for staff committees, orchestrating tasks, and coordinating all operational functions. The Holy Spirit does all these and more. ***He leads, directs, guides, and coordinates all things to work exactly as they should for the good of believers and for the purposes of His Kingdom (John 16:13; Rom. 8:14; Rom. 8:28).***

3. **The Holy Spirit "Steers" the "Ship of Zion."**
   As mentioned on page 43, administrators are like the ***helmsmen of ships***; they ***steer*** the ship to arrive at the destination set by the captain. The "Captain" is Jesus, the head of the Church. It's His Church, not ours, and He determines all that we must accomplish to fulfill His purposes and arrive at our destination. How, then, does Jesus communicate His will to us? ***It's through the Holy Spirit! Because He is "God-in-our-hearts," He brings Scripture alive and reveals to church leaders Christ's intentions (Col. 1:17-18; John 15:26; Eph. 4:11-16).***

4. **The Holy Spirit Gives Assignments.**
   Just as an administrator gives staff and committee assignments, so does the Holy Spirit. ***When men and women are called to specific works, it's the Holy Spirit who activates their call (Rom. 1:1; Gal. 1:15). The Holy Spirit sets people apart, equips them, and sends them out to fulfill their assignments (Acts 13:2-5).***

5. **The Holy Spirit Sets Up Divine Appointments.**
   An administrator arranges and sets up appointments for both company personnel and clients. ***The Holy Spirit supernaturally arranges divine appointments for the on-going work of God's Kingdom. (Paul and Ananias – Acts chapter 9; Peter and Cornelius - Acts chapter 10.)***

6. **The Holy Spirit Makes Course Adjustments When Needed.**
   Part of the oversight responsibilities of an administrator is adjusting the assignments of staff and committees. ***This is what the Holy Spirit did when He redirected Paul's ministry from Bithynia to Macedonia (Acts 16:6-10).***

VII - Epilogue: Renewing Our Emphasis on the Holy Spirit

It's my prayer that this brief book has brought a fresh understanding and reminder of the Power and Ministry of the Holy Spirit in the world, in your personal life, in the church, and in God's Kingdom. As a teacher of God's word, I cannot just present biblical truth without practical ways to live out our faith in the world. In other words, I answer the question, **"WHAT THEN SHALL WE DO?"**

Here Are Some Thoughts on How We Can Renew Our Emphasis on the Holy Spirit.

1. **Do Your Own Personal Studies on the Holy Spirit.**

   It's one thing to go to a restaurant and order food that has already been harvested, prepared and cooked. But it's a totally different matter to grow your own food, cook it, and store some away for the winter. Instead of just letting the pastor do your Bible studies for you, study God's word for yourself! ***When you search the Scriptures for passages that give you understanding of the Holy Spirit's work in your life, it will be locked in your heart for as long as you live.***

2. **Journal What the Holy Spirit Is Doing in Your Life and Speaking to Your Heart.**

   Many years ago, I created a folder on my computer entitled, **"What the Holy Spirit Is Saying to Me."** Then year by year I make entries of what He has done and the things I have prayed for. This doesn't have to be a daily record, but it should be consistent. ***Then, when you review your journal to see all that the Lord has done, it builds your faith and encourages you for future challenges in your life.***

3. **Attend Ministry Settings Where the Gifts of the Holy Spirit Are Alive and Flowing.**

   There's nothing more electrifying than being in a ministry environment where the Holy Spirit is supernaturally working real-time in peoples' lives. When we receive a word directly from the Lord or a healing touch from Him, it stirs our faith and moves us deeper into His Kingdom. ***When this happens, the Holy Spirit will forever be in the forefront of your heart and mind.***

4. **If You're a Church Leader, Preach, and Teach the Reality of the Holy Spirit's Work in People's Lives.**

   To bring biblically sound messages to your congregation, it requires diligent prayer, research, collaborative reading, and comprehensive Bible studies. ***The more you preach and teach on the Holy Spirit, the more important He becomes in your own life...and the more time you will give in your services for the Gifts of the Spirit to flow.***

5. **In Our Modern Age of Technology, On-line Church Services and Conferences, Don't Forget the Holy Spirit!**

   What a blessing it is to peach, teach, and minister to people through the amazing advent of Internet Technology. For those who are homebound with age, sicknesses, or injuries, they not isolated from our ministries. ***However, as Archbishop Kirby Clements often reminds us, though we use technology, we can never become overdependent upon it. Regardless of the convenience of the Internet, our confidence and total dependency is fully on the Person, Power, and Ministry of the Holy Spirit. Without Him, our ministries degenerate down to just public talks on topical ideas!***

6. **Pray in the Spirit...Often!**

   Praying in the Holy Spirit (with your spiritual prayer language) draws you deeper and closer into who He is and what God's intentions are. ***As covered on pages 24 and 32, praying in the Holy Spirit aligns your life with God's will, and prophetically reveals to you the mysteries of the Kingdom of God.***

7. **Finally, Obey the "Still Small Voice" of the Holy Spirit "Whispering" in Your Spirit and Heart!**

   God is always speaking to us. Our problem is that it's difficult to slow down our hectic lives long enough to hear what He's saying. And then, even if we do sense the Holy Spirit's voice, it can easily be placed on the "back burners" of our lives. ***He's trying to lead us, direct us, and guard us from hidden dangers that can ruin our souls. If we don't listen and obey, disastrous consequences may befall us (Is. 48:17-19 NIV).***

Other Books Written by Pastor Dan Rhodes

Books are listed from the earliest to the latest.
Most are available on Amazon.
For Questions, Email: DanCRhodes@DestinyNavigators.org

SETTING YOUR HEART ON THE KINGDOM *(12 BOOKS)*

A 12-book daily devotional series on the Kingdom of God from every book of the Bible for each day of the year (365 devotionals) with practical applications for life.

NAVIGATING THE UNCHARTED WATERS OF YOUR DESTINY *(TWO WORKBOOKS)*

A Workbook Study Guide Series - Helping people discover and live in their God-called destinies with personal applications.

NAVIGATING LIFE WITH GOD'S COMPASS

A Spiritual Navigational Guide - Biblical Teachings from each of the 66 books of the Bible with practical Life-Navigational insights.

PURSUING GOD'S KINGDOM ABOVE ALL ELSE

A "fill-in-the-blank" teaching manual on how to seek first the Kingdom of God. This includes both **Teacher** and **Student** Editions for study groups and classes.

ONCE UPON A KINGDOM

A Spiritual Allegory of God's Kingdom set on the backdrop of Medieval Kings, Kingdoms, Knights, Evil Rulers and Dragons. This is written with the younger generation in mind.

TOUGH QUESTIONS YOU'RE AFRAID TO ASK YOUR PASTOR

Thirty Challenging Questions about the Bible, Life, and Ministry answered from God's Word. Plus, practical points for each teaching asking, "What does each answer really mean to you?"

THE LOGOS OF THE KINGDOM

A comprehensive Theological Summary of God, His Eternal Kingdom and Victorious Church with over 3,300 Scripture References. It clearly describes what the Message of the Kingdom **IS** and is **NOT** with Practical Applications. You'll learn that the Kingdom of God isn't a theoretical concept; it's eternal reality.

SEASONS IN TIME

A ministry anthology of true-to-life vignettes of people who encountered God Face to Face in different seasons of life. Those who responded to God's visitations lived restored and fulfilled lives. Perhaps the "Story of Your Life" is like one of these.

GOD'S COUNTERCULTURE

A person without a life-strategy is like a ship without a compass or rudder, drifting with the prevailing winds of society's ever-changing mores. This book reveals how we should live so that

God's Culture is infused in our hearts and minds to transform the world around us.

DISCOVERING THE ANCIENT PATHS

One-Minute Devotionals from each book of the Bible, Genesis to Revelation. If you'd like to know what God thinks and feels about you, the Ancient Paths will lead you there. Ancient Paths pave the way to knowing how we should live, how God restores us, and how we discover our destiny in Him.

WHAT THEY DIDN'T TEACH ME IN SEMINARY

You'll read about true-life challenges that accompany pastoral ministry. But you'll also learn how to overcome them. You'll learn why pastors become discouraged and quit. You'll discover how to navigate challenges with both natural and spiritual solutions.

DEVELOPING A CHURCH-BASED SCHOOL OF CHRISTIAN MINISTRY

There is no greater accomplishment that satisfies a Christian Pastor more than imparting spiritual passion for God and ministry into the lives of people, who in turn influence others to do the same. This Handbook Includes:

- A Sensible Approach to Beginning a School of Ministry.
- Organizational Concepts.
- 1-year Certificate School of Practical Ministry.
- 2-year Associate Degree in Ministry.
- 4-year Degree Program in Ministry.
- Clearly Specified Course Offerings and Class Schedules

Made in the USA
Columbia, SC
01 February 2024